"As the church walks forward in the se
synodality on the local, regional, and u
for those who seek to turn this promis
fruitful harvest. Rooted in theological and historical foundations,
Kristin Colberg and Jos Moons move from the *what* of synodality
to the *how*, offering tools for cultivating the conversion of
attitudes, behaviors, structures, and practices to synodalize the
church's life and mission today."

—Sr. Nathalie Becquart, XMCJ, undersecretary
of the General Secretariat of the Synod

"This important book lives up to its claim to being both an
accessible explanation of the vision of a synodal church, as well
as a spiritual and practical guide to embedding that vision into
church life. Following the 2021–2024 Synod on Synodality, the
journey of 'synodalizing' the church will benefit greatly from this
hope-filled work. It is essential reading for those who wish to
understand the ongoing impacts of a truly synodal church."

—Ormond Rush, Australian Catholic University

"Colberg and Moons offer a rich testimony to the process of
the Synod on Synodality (2021–2024), rightly pointing to its
foundation in the Second Vatican Council's recovery of an
understanding of the shared dignity of all the baptized faithful,
their shared belonging to the pilgrim people of God, and co-
responsibility for the life and mission of the church. This book is
an indispensable resource for understanding the synod's aim of
helping us to become a truly synodal church in practice and for
receiving the orientations contained in its final document. It
should be required reading for bishops, pastors, deacons, lay
leaders, and all those preparing for ministry in the church today."

—Catherine E. Clifford, professor of systematic and historical
theology, Saint Paul University, Ottawa

"During the two synod sessions in Rome I experienced firsthand what it means to be a listening, participatory, and consultative church. And it was a deeply consoling experience that changed my understanding of the universal church. This superb new book is a wonderful resource to help people to begin, and continue, the synodal journey. It reminds us that synodality is a practice with deep historical roots and with solid theological foundations, and it offers concrete steps on how to move forward."

—James Martin, SJ, editor at large of America Media

"Synodality is a developing and all too often abstract term. In these early days, more work is needed to help us fully grasp its potential to transform our communities. This book expertly fills that gap. It offers a primer on the theological and historical origins of synodality while offering concrete suggestions for the attitudes, structures, and practices of personal and communal conversion required to unlock the radical possibilities of synodality to meet the needs of our hurting and rapidly changing world."

—Avril Braigent, facilitator at the Synod of Bishops, co-founder and director of the School for Synodality (UK)

"If synodality is 'journeying together,' I can think of no better guide along the way than this book. It's Rick Steves for the pilgrim people of God! Theologically grounded and pastorally realistic, Colberg and Moons provide an exemplary introduction to what is perhaps the most important development in the Catholic Church since the Second Vatican Council. It is simply the best single volume out there for understanding and advancing Pope Francis's vision of a more participatory, collaborative, and hopeful church."

—Edward P. Hahnenberg, Breen Chair for Catholic Systematic Theology, John Carroll University

The Future of Synodality

How We Move Forward from Here

Kristin M. Colberg and Jos Moons, SJ

LITURGICAL PRESS

Collegeville, Minnesota

litpress.org

Library of Congress Cataloging-in-Publication Data

Names: Colberg, Kristin, author. | Moons, Jos, 1980- author.
Title: The future of synodality : how we move forward from here / Kristin M. Colberg and Jos Moons, SJ.
Description: Collegeville, Minnesota : Liturgical Press, [2025] | Includes bibliographical references. | Summary: "In The Future of Synodality, readers are introduced to key aspects of the origins of synodality, its theological foundations, and recent expressions. In the second part, readers are encouraged to look towards the future and explore concrete transformations that can catalyze the on-going synodalization of the church-helping those engaged in the synodal process to better understand this historic moment in the church's life and learn how to walk together on the synodal path"-- Provided by publisher.
Identifiers: LCCN 2024038632 (print) | LCCN 2024038633 (ebook) | ISBN 9798400800160 (trade paperback) | ISBN 9798400800177 (epub) | ISBN 9780814689677 (pdf)
Subjects: LCSH: Catholic Church--Government. | Church renewal--Catholic Church.
Classification: LCC BX1746 .C537 2025 (print) | LCC BX1746 (ebook) | DDC 262/.02--dc23/eng/20241101
LC record available at https://lccn.loc.gov/2024038632
LC ebook record available at https://lccn.loc.gov/2024038633

Contents

Introduction

We live in an extraordinary time in the Catholic Church. Because we stand in the midst of it, it can be difficult to appreciate the distinctiveness of the present moment. The church has begun a profound process of renewal that engages every element of its life and its outreach to the world; it has embraced the path of synodality. Until recent years, the word *synodality* remained largely unfamiliar to many Catholics. While it sounds complex, it means something like "journeying together" (from the Greek *syn* = with, and *hodos* = road). Synodality is a way of being church that includes everyone, inviting all to speak and participate, appreciating the insights and gifts of each member of the community, seeking the way forward together. Most of all, it is a style "that starts from listening as the first act of the Church."[1]

Ecclesial synodality is both ancient and new. Like the Second Vatican Council (1962–1965) before it, the current process engages in both *ressourcement* (a return to the church's earliest sources) and *aggiornamento* (updating). Gathering in

---

1. General Secretariat for the Synod, *Instrumentum Laboris* for the Second Session of the 16th Ordinary General Assembly of the Synod of Bishops 6, July 9, 2024, https://www.synod.va/en/news/the-instrumentum-laboris.html. This text is referred to as *Instrumentum Laboris* 2024, to distinguish it from the *Instrumentum Laboris* written in service of the first general assembly in 2023, which can be found at https://www.synod.va/en/resources/documents /documents-for-the-second-phase/documents-for-the-1st-session-of-the-XVI -assembly/documents.html.

synods began in the earliest days of the church and has continued as a vital tool of consensus-building over the last two millennia. These moments of collaborative decision-making where Christians (usually bishops) gathered to pray, listen, dialogue, and discern ways forward for the church stand out as major moments of the church's life. Today, the church wants to embrace essential aspects of these gatherings while updating them to involve the participation of the entire People of God and meet the needs of a global church today. The church also finds itself confronted with unprecedented challenges that extend across the entire world, such as a wide range of violent conflicts, a looming climate crisis, the widening gap in economic equality and opportunity, and growing political polarization. In the face of the significant complexities facing the church and the world, the Catholic Church has committed itself in recent years to the synodal path because it believes that it is what God "expects of the Church of the third millennium."[2]

To explore this style of being church, the Catholic Church undertook the Synod on Synodality (2021–2024). As we will see in this book, the synodal way ushered many welcome innovations into being. By engaging in the "greatest consultation effort in human history," the church listened to and with the People of God to discern the call of the Holy Spirit.[3] At the very beginning of the process, the official guidebook stated: "This Synod aims to promote a new style of living out the

2. Pope Francis, Ceremony Commemorating the 50th Anniversary of the Institution of the Synod of Bishops, October 17, 2015, https://www.vatican .va/content/francesco/en/speeches/2015/october/documents/papa -francesco_20151017_50-anniversario-sinodo.html.

3. Christopher Lamb, "Pope Francis Announces Global Synod Meeting Will Occur Over Two Years," *Chicago Catholic*, October 19, 2022, https:// www.chicagocatholic.com/vatican/-/article/2022/10/19/pope-francis -announces-global-synod-meeting-will-occur-over-two-years.

communion, participation, and mission of the Church."[4] Now that the Synod on Synodality has ended, the question of how we can *continue* to grow in this new, more synodal—more inclusive, participative, humble, and spiritual—ecclesial style remains. This book wants to contribute to the conversation on that question.

It wants to do so in two unique ways. First, this is a comprehensive presentation that is complete without getting lost in the details. Instead of focusing on one aspect, we address various dimensions: history, theology, concrete aspects of the Synod 2021–24, types of behavior that befit synodality, and ecclesial structures. Second, this is a readable and accessible book. In order to truly journey together, as synodality requires, it is important that everyone has a sense of the nature and aims of synodality. Unfortunately, the (many!) theological articles and books on synodality are often not very accessible. The writing style may be too dense, the length may be discouraging, or the content may be too abstract or specialized. While we need those types of materials, they need to be complemented with solid yet accessible presentations of a more general kind at the service of all of the People of God. That is what this book hopes to achieve.

The book consists of two parts. In part one, we survey the developments of the last several years, during which much has happened. It should clarify matters to those who are interested but not too sure about what's happening or who have some suspicions. It aims to help those who don't see the forest for the trees and those who see some trees but can't identify the forest. We discuss four aspects, the first of which is theology. It is important to underscore that synodality has deep theological roots, especially in the Second Vatican Council.

---

4. General Secretariat for the Synod, *Vademecum* for the Synod on Synodality 3.5, September 7, 2021, https://www.synod.va/en/news/the-vademecum-for-the-synod-on-synodality.html.

The theological exploration in the first chapter is complemented by a historical exploration in the second chapter. We will see that synodality can be traced back as far as the Acts of the Apostles. Moreover, it is a fitting (and necessary) response to contemporary crises such as the sexual abuse scandal and the cover-up culture. Pope Francis's role in inspiring synodality is mentioned, too. In the third and fourth chapters, we focus on the Synod 2021–24. Through a series of snapshots, we seek to bring to life the process as it unfolded, and then we move on to the topics that surfaced in the synodal deliberations in parishes, dioceses, countries, continents, and in Rome. These chapters are complemented by two appendixes with overviews of the major dates and major documents.

In part two, we look towards the future. The Synod 2021–24 was part of a much larger project, which is to develop synodality into the church's usual practice. This requires a "synodal conversion" or a "synodalization" of the church, that is, a wholesale change of thinking, acting, and organizing ourselves to build up a church that is marked by synodality. What does the church need to move forward in that direction? We point to three challenges, pertaining to synodal *attitudes and behavior*, synodal *structures*, and synodal *practices*. Chapter five presents these challenges and explains how they complement one another. Chapter six focuses on attitudes and behavior of the faithful—all of us. How can we become better listeners? How can we become better at journeying together? Chapter seven looks into the way we organize ourselves in the church: our procedures, rules, and structures. How can ecclesial structures, rules, and processes better reflect a participative and inclusive church, and better contribute to it? Finally, the last chapter explores practices: the realm of culture and habits, which typically situates itself in between behavior, which is highly personal, and structures, which are highly impersonal. What would a synodal culture look like? By way of a case study, we delve into an ancient example, the monastic communities rooted in the Rule of Saint Benedict.

Immediately after the Second Vatican Council, the influential German theologian Karl Rahner wrote a small booklet titled "The Council: A New Beginning."[5] The council, Rahner knew, was not the end point but rather the beginning of something. Like Vatican II, so the Synod 2021–24 is a new beginning, too. This book hopes to contribute to that new beginning.

This book has been coauthored by Kristin Colberg (College of Saint Benedict and Saint John's University and School of Theology and Seminary, Collegeville, MN) and Jos Moons, SJ (KU Leuven, Belgium, and Boston College), who both have extensive experience with the topic. Trusting that our experiences and talents would be complementary, we decided to write the book together. We have extensively discussed each chapter, and while our different styles are still noticeable, the content belongs to both of us. In so doing, we felt we were doing what we were writing about: journeying together, learning from one another, appreciating one another for what we think and are.

Kristin Colberg was a member of the Theological Commission advising the Synod on Synodality 2021–24. As such she was involved in many aspects of the preparation for it. One of her most notable contributions is that she served as a member of the writing team that produced the Working Document for the Continental Stage, Enlarge the Space of Your Tent. She also collaborated extensively with the United States Conference of Catholic Bishops and the Diocese of Saint Cloud, Minnesota, during the local and regional phases of the synod. During the three years of the Synod on Synodality, she traveled

5. Karl Rahner, SJ, "The Council: A New Beginning," in *The Church after the Council*, trans. D. C. Herron and R. Albrecht (New York: Herder & Herder, 1966), 9–33.

across the United States to several countries, participating in listening sessions and speaking about the synod. Kristin is also a member of the Anglican-Roman Catholic International Commission, which has also taught her the ways of synodal walking together.

Jos Moons was the main researcher for a research project entitled "Mapping Synodality," which reviewed academic publications on the synod and on synodality. The fruits thereof include an academic bibliography for the period 2013–2024, covering English, French, German, and Spanish literature, and a series of theological briefing papers that provided short, accessible summaries of the academic conversation on key topics such as participation, the role of the bishop in a synodal church, the participation of women, and canon law. He has published scholarly articles on synodality in Dutch, English, French, Italian, and Spanish in which he has discussed the baptismal foundation of synodality, attitudes such as listening, practices such as discernment of spirits, the Holy Spirit as the synod's protagonist, and canon law and its limitations. He edited the book *Witnesses of Synodality: Good Practices and Experiences* (Paulist Press, 2024).

We would like to express our thanks to Hans Christoffersen, who first suggested writing a book for Liturgical Press. Thanks also to the monks of Saint John's Abbey, who have been so kind to host me (Jos) for a time of undisturbed writing. Thanks to Barry Hudock, who has reviewed our texts with great dedication and professionalism. Deep gratitude is also extended to Shawn Colberg, who read many chapters of this book and provided invaluable comments, editing and insight.

Part I

Synodality

Foundations and Recent Developments

Chapter One

Why Synodality?

Theological Considerations

The Catholic Church today has committed itself to a synodal path. It seeks to develop a new way of proceeding that is characterized by listening, consultation, and dialogue. The point is to seek the way forward *together*. Building up the church and serving our neighbors is done together: all can contribute and participate. One reason this is a good idea is that this way of being church reflects sound theological convictions. Listening to our fellow Christians is ultimately a matter of faith: we believe that the Holy Spirit speaks to us through our brothers and sisters. Similarly, appreciating the contributions of every member of the community also has a deep theological foundation, as it is a way of honoring each person's gifts, which are ultimately given by the Spirit. This chapter explores several theological notions that are foundational for synodality.[1]

---

1. What follows adapts some ideas and material from Jos Moons, SJ, "A Comprehensive Introduction to Synodality: Reconfiguring Ecclesiology and Ecclesial Practice," *Roczniki Teologiczne (Annals of Theology)* 69/2 (2022): 73–93.

The Second Vatican Council, which also sought to reform the church, will play a key role in these reflections. Vatican II promoted a church that preaches the Gospel by convincing, not imposing, and it set first steps on the path of appreciating the wisdom found in other churches and, indeed, in society. Dialogue was not only embraced as the council's style, but it was also promoted as the church's style in general. In terms of content, the council elaborated various notions that are central to the synodal process, such as the People of God, *sensus fidelium*, charisms, journeying, and style. In many ways, current efforts to promote synodality can be seen as efforts to advance the council's teaching. Explaining the synod's theological foundation can, therefore, not be done without unpacking the council. Official documents for the synod explicitly make this connection. For example, the Synthesis Report 2023 speaks of the Synod 2021–24 as "a true act of further reception of the Council, prolonging its inspiration and reinvigorating its prophetic force for today's world."[2] In other words, synodality takes up crucial elements from the council, shaping them in a way that befits the contemporary context.

Baptism and the People of God

We ourselves, the faithful, constitute a first foundation for synodality. To use an image of Pope Francis: synodality inverts the ecclesial pyramid and starts with all of us. The importance of the faithful in the life of the church is evident in the way the Synod 2021–24 functioned. For example, the synodal

---

2. Synthesis Report: A Synodal Church in Mission (hereafter: Synthesis Report 2023), Introduction, https://www.synod.va/content/dam/synod /assembly/synthesis/english/2023.10.28-ENG-Synthesis-Report.pdf. Cf. 1a: "The Second Vatican Council 'updated' this [synodal] practice [of the early church], and Pope Francis once again encouraged the Church to renew it. The Synod 2021–2024 is part of this renewal."

process opened with a consultation that sought to include all the faithful. According to the Working Document for the Continental Stage (2022), in which the views of participants in this consultation were gathered, "many emphasized that this was the first time the Church had asked for their opinion and they wish to continue this journey."[3] Another strong indication that believers other than bishops were being taken seriously is the fact that a (limited) number of lay people, including women, fully participated in the 2023 synod meeting, with the right both to speak and to vote, and that there were lay facilitators, again including women.[4]

The theological foundation of this innovation is the sacrament of baptism.[5] All the faithful share the fundamental, equal dignity of being baptized. While that dignity bears resemblance to the fundamental human dignity shared by all people, whatever their faith, it has a deeper and more explicitly Christian layer also. Ultimately, that is a mystical layer. In baptism, we have been clothed with Christ, anointed with the Holy Spirit, and confirmed in our adoptive daughter- and sonship by God the Father.

3. General Secretariat for the Synod, Working Document for the Continental Stage, Enlarge the Space of Your Tent 16, https://www.synod.va /content/dam/synod/common/phases/continental-stage/dcs/Documento-Tappa-Continentale-EN.pdf (hereafter cited as Document for the Continental Stage).

4. The Synod of Bishops 2023 had 364 participants with the right to speak and to vote, plus the pope. Of those, 54 were women (29 lay women and 25 religious women) and 27 were priests. In addition, there were 85 facilitators and experts. See Antoine Mekary's "Here's the Synod in Key Numbers," October 5, 2023, https://aleteia.org/2023/10/05/heres-the -synod-in-key-numbers/.

5. On baptism as a foundation for synodality, see Jos Moons, SJ, "Broadening the Baptismal Foundation of a Synodal Church: A Plea for a Baptismal Ethos," *Studia Canonica* 58 (2024): 131–52; see also Susan K. Wood, SCL, ed., *Ordering the Baptismal Priesthood: Theologies of Lay and Ordained Ministry* (Collegeville, MN: Liturgical Press, 2003).

The sacrament of baptism also has an ecclesial significance: through it, one becomes part of the Christian community. While in modern Western contexts, the celebration of baptism sometimes functions as a religious version of a baby shower, originally it was the end point of a long process of personal and spiritual development with a step-by-step introduction to the faith community. In theological terms, baptism makes one part of the People of God. For, as *Lumen Gentium* beautifully states, God does not want us to be saved individually but connected with one another, as a people (see LG 9).

While this baptismal dignity is a grace, it also comes with responsibilities, namely, to contribute to the building up of the kingdom of God and of the church by words and deeds, by prayer and action. Two theological terms help to specify this ecclesial responsibility, namely, *sensus fidelium* and charisms. The *sensus fidelium* is an instinct for the truth that all the faithful, including those without theological training, have. It is sometimes described as an "innate sense," an intuition for what is true about God, faith, church. On the one hand, the notion of *sensus fidelium* is an act of faith in God working in and through all of the faithful, not just the professionals, be it theologians or clergy. Theological reflection speaks of that instinct as a fruit of the Holy Spirit working in us and, therefore, as something that is freely given. On the other hand, we should avoid identifying all that comes to our mind or heart as the voice of God; of course, it may just be our own imagination, the influence of the culture we live in, or even our human sinfulness that is at work. Therefore, we can and should develop or refine that faith instinct by living a life of faith in God and prayer, serving our neighbor, engaging in fraternal conversations with fellow Christians (and people in general), and theological formation.

Ideally, we should hope for faith intuitions shared by all, for if we reach consensus, we can be sure that God is at work in us. As *Lumen Gentium* puts it, "The whole body of the faithful who have received an anointing which comes from the holy one (see 1 Jn 2:20 and 27) cannot be mistaken in belief" (LG 12).[6] Since our diversity is such that unanimity is improbable, a more pragmatic perspective may be more useful. Practically speaking, the implication of the *sensus fidelium* is that dialogue is important. Members of the faithful need to make their voices—or rather, their faith witness—heard. At the same time, they need to listen to other voices. Just like the Spirit may be speaking through me, he may be speaking through somebody else. Especially for church leaders and theologians, that is a challenge. Having been trained and missioned to teach, they are sometimes less familiar with listening to and learning from "ordinary faithful" outside of their own circles, be it academic or episcopal, who don't "speak their language." Once again, the faith intuitions of these "ordinary faithful" may actually be very instructive—it may be that God's Spirit speaks through them.

Another way to contribute to the building up of the kingdom of God and of the church are to use our charisms. Charisms are gifts that God gives to each person, to equip her or him to build up the church and the kingdom. Here St. Paul's image of the one body with a variety of members—read gifts and graces—is helpful (see 1 Cor 12–14). People have different gifts. These should not lead to haughty self-congratulation, rivalry, or fights, as easily happens, both in Corinth almost two thousand years ago and in our own parishes today. Instead, one should employ one's gifts in such a way that they serve others and, in case of doubt, aim for the highest gift, which is love.[7] Paul's exhortation means that we all have something to give to the other members of the body and that we all receive something

6. All quotations from the documents of the Second Vatican Council are taken from Austin Flannery, OP, ed., *Vatican Council II: Constitutions, Decrees, Declarations; The Basic Sixteen Documents* (Collegeville, MN: Liturgical Press, 2014).

7. Note that the canticle of love in 1 Cor 13 is often read at weddings but is not about romantic love.

as well, and this is a key concept of synodality. That something may be the spiritual gifts that St. Paul refers to, but it may also be our experiences, insights, and thoughts.

The Second Vatican Council sees these charisms as gifts from the Spirit and contends that, by means of them, the Spirit seeks to build up the church. To say the same thing in more critical terms: building up the church is not only a matter of hierarchical ministry; all the faithful have a role to play. That is the starting point of *Lumen Gentium*'s teaching on charisms: "It is not only through the sacraments and the ministries that the holy Spirit makes the people holy, leads them and enriches them with his virtues. Allotting his gifts 'at will to each individual' (1 Cor 12:11), he also distributes special graces among the faithful of every rank. By these gifts he makes them fit and ready to undertake various tasks and offices for the renewal and building up of the church" (LG 12). Practically, this means that we should all be active members of the church, as we all have gifts to share. Moreover, while contributing our bit, we should also acknowledge what others contribute and appreciate how we complement one another. A synodal church is participatory and appreciative.

The appreciation for our common baptismal dignity and for co-responsibility is grounded in several theological shifts or, in more technical language, reconfigurations. Reconfigurations are an important aspect of the Catholic approach to renewal. To go forward, we reach backward and seek a foundation in the past, thus providing renewal with theological validity. What we retrieve from history is presented—or "configured"—in such a way that newness emerges, for example, by shifting priorities. For instance, instead of starting with holy orders, synodality gives priority to baptism, recognizing it as the church's foundational sacrament. That is not to dismiss, downplay, or deny the importance of the sacrament of holy orders or the role of the ordained ministry in the life of the church; it means that these must be understood in the context of baptism. The church, its mission, and its unity are founded in the first place upon baptism, while ordained ministry is one way of carrying out that mission and serving that unity.

This reconfiguration in relation to our baptismal dignity takes up a crucial earlier reconfiguration carried out by the Second Vatican Council in the church's understanding of itself. While an early draft text of *Lumen Gentium*, the council's document on the church, had spoken first about the hierarchy (in chapter two) and then about "the People of God, especially the laity" (in chapter three), the final text speaks of the People of God as a whole in chapter two and then develops two specific groups within the church, the hierarchy (in chapter three) and the laity (in chapter four). Instead of imagining the church primarily according to distinctions based on higher and lower roles, the council wanted deliberately to start with the shared dignity that all of the faithful, the entire People of God, hold in common and that comes with a co-responsibility for the church's mission.[8] Accordingly, the Australian theologian Ormond Rush has rightly stated that one of the council's greatest achievements is the way that it gives us a vision of the church that is "primarily baptismal in orientation" rather than hierarchical in orientation.[9] Prioritizing baptism over ordination is an important step in taking up this theological shift and unlocking its potential for transforming the function of the church.

Another reconfiguration has to do with the appreciation of the *sensus fidelium* and of charisms. Synodality offers a more positive approach to these realities than has sometimes been the case. In the years since the council, magisterial documents have almost entirely "forgotten" the notion of *sensus fidelium*,

8. See the minutes of the council, *Acta synodalia Sacrosancti Concilii Vaticani II* (Vatican City: Typis Polyglottis Vaticanis, 1970–1999), vol. III/1, 209–10.

9. See Ormond Rush, "Inverting the Pyramid: The *Sensus Fidelium* in a Synodal Church," *Theological Studies* 78 (2017): 299–325.

focusing rather on magisterial teaching and obedience. This contrasts greatly with the extensive theological scholarship that has developed during this same period; indeed, publications on the topic have been so numerous that a series of overview articles was justified.[10] One sign of hope, however, is the publication of the study *Sensus Fidei* in the Life of the Church by the Vatican's International Theological Commission in 2014.[11]

Similarly, magisterial documents have tended to narrow down charisms by linking them with specific groups in the church, especially those belonging to the charismatic renewal or the so-called new movements. They have often stressed that the laity's responsibility is particularly to build up the kingdom, leaving the running of the church for the most part to the clergy. Church documents tended to warn against lay clericalization. Synodality takes a different approach and revisits the broader notion of charisms as found in the writings of St. Paul and in *Lumen Gentium*. In so doing, synodality is an important step forward in developing a more generous appreciation of the essential contribution of the lay faithful.

Third and finally, these theological reconfigurations also affect our understanding of ecclesial leadership.[12] Certainly hierarchical leadership remains. In a synodal church, bishops

10. See John J. Burkhard, OFM Conv, "*Sensus Fidei:* Theological Reflection Since Vatican II: Part I: 1965–1984," *The Heythrop Journal* 34 (1993): 41–59; "*Sensus Fidei:* Theological Reflection Since Vatican II: Part II: 1985–1989," *The Heythrop Journal* 34 (1993): 123–36; "*Sensus Fidei:* Recent Theological Reflection (1990–2001): Part I," *The Heythrop Journal* 46 (2005): 450–75; "*Sensus Fidei:* Recent Theological Reflection (1990–2001): Part II," *The Heythrop Journal* 47 (2006): 38–54.

11. International Theological Commission, *Sensus Fidei* in the Life of the Church (2014), https://www.vatican.va/roman_curia/congregations/cfaith/cti_documents/rc_cti_20140610_sensus-fidei_en.html.

12. See the seminal article by Myriam Wijlens, "Reforming the Church by Hitting the Reset Button: Reconfiguring Collegiality within Synodality because of *sensus fidei fidelium*," *The Canonist* 8 (2017): 235–61.

continue to fulfil an important role. Anointed by the Spirit, missioned by Christ, and appointed by the pope, their task is to shepherd their flock, in collegial collaboration and communion with their fellow bishops and other pastors. In a synodal church, too, bishops and the pope have the final word. The major shift here is that prior to having the final word, leaders should listen and learn. Bishops, priests, deacons, religious superiors, and other church leaders should become team players who welcome advice, encourage initiatives, share their considerations and decisions, and so on. Thus, rather than focusing on their authority, they should focus on processes of consultation, dialogue, collaboration, and complementarity.

Therefore, distinctions such as that between higher and lower members of the church—a distinction one still finds in *Lumen Gentium* and that underpins ecclesial titles such as "Your Eminence"—no longer make sense, for our highest dignity is a common one.[13] The first reality of the church is what we are together: the People of God. This holds a particular significance for the magisterium and its teaching role. In a synodal church, the magisterium, too, is learning. As Francis said in his notable 2015 address on synodality: "Everyone has something to learn. The faithful people, the college of bishops, the Bishop of Rome: all listening to each other, and all listening to the Holy Spirit, the 'Spirit of truth' (Jn 14:17), in order to know what he 'says to the Churches' (Rev 2:7)."[14] Thus, the church is a *communio*, as post-conciliar magisterial teaching has emphasized, but we should not stress the hierarchical aspect of the church (the *communio hierarchica*) but rather the communion of the faithful.

13. For that distinction, cf. what *Lumen Gentium* teaches on the ordained and non-ordained "differ[ing] essentially and not only in degree" (LG 9), thus taking up the old idea that the ordained are "more important" members of the church.

14. Pope Francis, Ceremony Commemorating the 50th Anniversary.

A Journeying and Learning Church

A second foundation is the metaphor of being on a journey. It implies that we have not yet reached our destination. A journeying church acknowledges itself as unfinished. The metaphor implies that the church is not a static reality but a dynamic one that continues to unfold. A journeying church accepts that its voyage involves encounters, unexpected events, surprises, and disappointments, for experience teaches that journeys usually involve all of these elements. From a faith perspective, it is God who guides our way, and a journeying church is eager to know where God is leading it.

The Second Vatican Council regularly speaks about a journeying church. One important way it does is through its use of the Latin root *peregrin-*, which refers to journeying or being on pilgrimage. Journeys or pilgrimages are, of course, sometimes not exciting or pleasant. For the church to *peregrinari* is to undertake the arduous journey of those who are not yet in heaven and who experience that through the trials and tribulations that they are undergoing. *Lumen Gentium* calls the church an *ecclesia perigrinans*, a "pilgrim church" (see the title of its chapter seven), and it teaches, "While on earth [the church] journeys [*peregrinatur*] in a foreign land away from the Lord" (LG 6). The tone is somewhat somber: "a foreign land" and "away from the Lord."

Conciliar thinking about the church's journeying is also expressed in three other ways. In the first place, *Lumen Gentium* presents the church as journeying towards something that it has not reached yet, using various terms to refer to its destination: the end of times, the new heavens and the new earth, being with Christ or with the Father, and so on (see LG 2, LG 48, or GS 1). Sometimes the text hints at the church's unfinished-ness. For example, LG 48 states that the church's outward aspect does not have perennial value but belongs to this age: "The pilgrim Church, in its sacraments and institutions, which belong to this present age, carries the mark of this world which will pass, and it takes its place among the creatures which groan and until now suffer the pains of childbirth and await the revelation of the children of God." The church has not yet reached its destination, and its journey is a humble one, all the more so as it owes its origin also to God. The document's opening section specifies that Christ is the light of the peoples, with the church being called to pass on that light. In the subsequent sections, it situates the church in the context of the Father's plan of salvation, the Son's execution of that plan, and the Spirit's sanctifying presence (LG 2–4). Thus, the church is part of a bigger plan that it does not "master." In synodal terms, all of this means that the church has to be listening to God's voice and accepting his leadership on the journey.

The church's journeying is also expressed in terms of time and history. While journeying from God and towards the end of times, the church is situated in time. Commentators like Giuseppe Alberigo, John W. O'Malley, and Giuseppe Ruggieri have each pointed out that the council was introducing a new idea when it imagined the church as *part* of history rather than solely *above* or *beyond* history.[15] This means that faith practice and faith formulations are always, as Ormond Rush puts it, "necessarily and inevitably conditioned by the particularities of time and place."[16] That leads us to what is arguably one of the key missions of the council: updating the church's expression of its faith so that it would be meaningful in the current time and place.

For example, in his famous opening address to the council, *Gaudet Mater Ecclesia*, Pope John XXIII explained to the

---

15. See Ormond Rush, *The Vision of Vatican II: Its Fundamental Principles* (Collegeville, MN: Liturgical Press, 2019), 165–87; this is the section on the principle "Faith/History."

16. Rush, *Vision of Vatican II*, 174.

council fathers that the church's expression of its faith needed to be updated so that its attractiveness would be more apparent. To make that happen, the council fathers should simultaneously honor the past and take seriously modern times. In the pope's own words: "It is first of all necessary that the Church never turn her eyes from the sacred heritage of truth which she has received from those who went before; and at the same time she must also look at the present times which have introduced new conditions and new forms of life, and have opened new avenues for the Catholic apostolate."[17]

The spirit of these words would develop into the double program of revisiting our sources (*ressourcement*) and unpacking them in dialogue with the reality of modern times (*aggiornamento*).[18] This way of proceeding is opposed to a traditionalist perspective, which holds fast only to what has been formulated and done in the past. John XXIII was aware of that mentality and therefore warned against treating the treasure of the faith as if it were a museum piece—an "*antiquitas.*" Instead, the council needed to interpret the treasure of faith anew in the context of modern times. So, too, does synodality.

In the third place, being situated in history is not only a limitation but can also be a grace. That is what the notion of "signs of the times" tries to say: God can speak to us through events. Evidently, these events do not automatically speak of God and need further discernment in light of the Gospel. What is new, however, is the positive attitude towards culture and context: they may be the starting point for new insights. Typical examples of positive cultural developments from which the church has learned include the civil recognition of

17. Joseph A. Komonchak, "*Gaudet Mater Ecclesia*: Pope John's Opening Speech to the Council," https://jakomonchak.files.wordpress.com /2012/10/john-xxiii-opening-speech.pdf.

18. See Rush, *Vision of Vatican II*, 17–21; this is the section on the principle "Ressourcement/Aggiornamento."

religious freedom, the rise of ecumenism, feminism, and—
more recently—ecology; in all cases, the church has recognized
what was happening in society as valuable and true from a
Gospel perspective also.[19] Taking into account the signs of the
times is certainly a challenge, for we need to generously welcome such signs as possible messengers from God, without
confusing them with the *Zeitgeist*.

In summary, a journeying church relates to time in various
ways. It acknowledges that it is on its way to the final goal and
therefore unfinished. It is conditioned by the particular time in
which it is situated and therefore needs constantly to find the
best way to speak to the here and now—*aggiornamento*. Finally,
developments in time may be instrumental in calling the church
to a new faithfulness to the Gospel, such as in the case of religious freedom, ecumenism, or ecology; here God is communi-
cating through time-bound events—the signs of the times.
These three elements make up a robust theological foundation
for a synodal church that is "together on the way." A synodal
church is eager to learn and to grow, seeks to be relevant and
meaningful here and now, and takes into account what happens
around it and how it may learn from these events.

The prominence of journeying as a metaphor for the life of
the church represents an important shift in the use of ecclesial
metaphors. In the late nineteenth and early twentieth centuries, an institutional model of the church predominated
Catholic understanding, with a focus on visible elements, especially the Creed, the pope, and the sacraments. In the
course of the twentieth century, other models have come to
the fore, stressing the transcendental dimension of the church
(Mystical Body), the mediating function of the church (sacrament), or the communitarian dimension of the church (People

19. Rush quotes John Courtney Murray commenting that "in all honesty
it must be admitted that the Church is late in acknowledging the validity
of the principle [of religious freedom]." Rush, *Vision of Vatican II*, 184.

of God).[20] Evidently, these metaphors complement one another, with no single one being able to capture the full richness of the church.[21] The exact way in which that complementarity is elaborated depends on one's theological priorities. A synodal time favors a humble, dynamic, and open imagination of the church—a journeying and learning church.

Pope Francis captured this dynamic notion of a journeying church when he addressed the faithful of the Diocese of Rome at the beginning of the synodal journey. He spoke of "seeking answers in God's revelation through a pilgrim hermeneutic capable of persevering in the journey begun in the Acts of the Apostles." With that, he meant to say that the church must interpret tradition in dialogue with what is going on here and now, as the church has always done. He then stressed the importance of keeping moving by speaking about the Spirit and about stagnant water: "Once the Church stops, she is no longer Church, but a lovely pious association, for she keeps the Holy Spirit in a cage. . . . Unless water keeps flowing, it becomes stagnant and putrefies. A stagnant Church starts to decay."[22]

The Holy Spirit as "The Great Protagonist"

In the third place, synodality is built on the conviction that the Holy Spirit actively guides the church. The ultimate leader of the church is neither the pope, the cardinals, nor the People of God—it is the Holy Spirit. Unfortunately, in our descriptions of synodality, the Spirit's crucial role sometimes remains

---

20. For these and other metaphors, see Avery Dulles, SJ, *Models of the Church* (New York: Doubleday, 2022 [orig. ed. 1974]).

21. For Dulles's comments on the church as a mysterious reality and on the importance of broad, catholic thinking, see Dulles, *Models of the Church*, 2–3.

22. Pope Francis, Address to the Faithful of the Diocese of Rome, September 18, 2021, https://www.vatican.va/content/francesco/en/speeches/2021/september/documents/20210918-fedeli-diocesiroma.html.

implicit. For example, the common shorthand explanation of synodality as a church that is "walking together" does not make mention of the Spirit. This risks losing sight of the fact that the church walks together "in order to listen to the Spirit" or "while listening to the Spirit." For synodality is not just about the church but also about God. The communal aspect of the synodal adventure cannot be understood properly without the transcendent, pneumatological dimension.

This third foundation has less basis in conciliar teaching. While the council did not forget the Spirit, its documents typically have a strong focus on Christ. Even when the Spirit is mentioned, it is often in reference to Christ: "his Spirit," "the Spirit of Christ," or the Spirit as the instrument through which Christ works. In those texts the Spirit is always linked to Christ and even situated under Christ. Noteworthy, too, are phrases such as "unity in the Holy Spirit," where the Spirit describes the noun *unity*. The resulting impression is that the Spirit is important as an afterthought, to add further details or precision, without being essential. One may think of the Spirit as a VIP seated in the second row—with Christ and the Father seated in the first row. The trinitarian introduction in *Lumen Gentium* 2–4 and the bold statements on the Spirit in the teachings of *Lumen Gentium* 12 on charisms and the *sensus fidelium* are the exceptions that prove the rule.[23]

By contrast, in Pope Francis's comments about synodality, the Spirit is clearly given a seat in the first row; Francis is keenly aware of the importance of the Spirit.[24] Both the frequency

---

23. See Jos Moons, SJ, *The Holy Spirit, the Church, and Pneumatological Renewal:* Mystici Corporis, Lumen Gentium *and Beyond* (Leiden and Boston: Brill, 2022).

24. For a scholarly elaboration of what follows here, see Jos Moons, SJ, "The Holy Spirit as the Protagonist of the Synod: Pope Francis's Creative Reception of the Second Vatican Council," *Theological Studies* 84/1 (2023): 61–78.

with which he speaks about the Holy Spirit in relation to synodality and the form of his pneumatology stand out: he presents the Spirit as one who acts. For example, in his book-length interview with Austen Ivereigh, Francis stated, "What characterizes a synodal path is the role of the Holy Spirit. We listen, we discuss in groups, but above all we pay attention to what the Spirit has to say to us." The Spirit has agency; he speaks to us. Therefore, "we cannot speak of synodality unless we accept and live the presence of the Holy Spirit." Once again, this presence must be understood in an active manner. For example, looking back on the Synod on the Family, Francis noted, "Yet the Spirit saved us in the end, in a breakthrough at the close of the second meeting of the Synod on the Family."[25]

In addition to underscoring the Spirit's agency, these statements also hint at the Spirit's ultimate significance. Indeed, while each and every believer matters—we are all protagonists— the Spirit is "always the great 'protagonist' of the Church's life."[26] Therefore, a synodal church is characterized by a mutual listening that is also, and ultimately, about listening to the Spirit. This listening must be done without "predetermined agendas" and with an openness for what Francis calls "the new things of the Spirit," for "ours is a God of Surprises."[27] In the concluding homily for the Synod 2023, the pope spoke about "God's gratuitous and astonishing [*sorprendente*] love" and warned against "controlling God" so that he fits in our concepts and agenda.[28]

25. Pope Francis, *Let Us Dream: The Path to a Better Future* (London: Simon & Schuster, 2020), 85–88.

26. Pope Francis, Address to the Faithful of the Diocese of Rome.

27. Pope Francis, *Let Us Dream*, 93.

28. Pope Francis, Homily: Conclusion of the Ordinary General Assembly of the Synod of Bishops, October 29, 2023, https://www.vatican.va/content/francesco/en/homilies/2023/documents/20231029-omelia-conclusione-sinodo.html.

The importance of the Spirit is also evident in the so-called *Adsumus* prayer recommended in the official "Guidebook" (*Vademecum*) for the Synod 2021–24 and used at the beginning of each session of the 2023 and 2024 Synod of Bishops: "We stand before You, Holy Spirit, as we gather together in Your name. With You alone to guide us, make Yourself at home in our hearts. Teach us the way we must go and how we are to pursue it."[29] Liturgical scholar Martin Klöckener notes in a reflection on this prayer that addressing the Spirit directly is highly unusual for the Latin tradition but that it does characterize the Spanish Visigoth tradition.[30] Moreover, this prayer envisions a Holy Spirit who works quite actively, as one who dwells in us, guides us, and teaches us.

Texts like these are remarkable for their explicit focus on the Holy Spirit and the active articulation of his role. Most liturgical prayers address the Father, and most theological thinking focuses on Christ, with the Holy Spirit being forgotten or treated as secondary, for example, as Christ's instrument. Theologians have sometimes compared the Holy Spirit to Cinderella (whose two better-treated sisters got to go to the ball) or nickname the Spirit "the forgotten God" (the technical term is *Geistvergessenheit*). While theologians today disagree about whether this remains a problem, what is clear is that the pneumatological interpretation of God's agency in the *Adsumus* prayer and in Pope Francis's vision of synodality stands out.

Finally, a quick quantitative analysis confirms the synod's high level of interest in the Holy Spirit. For example, the

29. Full text available online at https://www.synod.va/en/resources/the -adsumus-prayer.html. For the *Vademecum*, see https://www.synod.va/en /news/the-vademecum-for-the-synod-on-synodality.html.

30. See Martin Klöckener, "La prière d'ouverture des conciles 'Adsumus': de l'Espagne wisigothique à la liturgie Romaine d'après Vatican II," in *La prière liturgique: Conférences Saint-Serge*, ed. Achille M. Triacca, SDB, and Alessandro Pistoia (Rome: Edizione Liturgiche, 2001), 179.

Preparatory Document (2021), which is meant to familiarize the church with the Vatican's take on synodality, refers to the Holy Spirit thirty-three times, with a very similar number of references to Christ (including Jesus and Lord).[31] Similarly, the Synthesis Report 2023 refers to the Holy Spirit forty-four times, with some sixty references to Christ (including Jesus and Lord).[32] It is unusual for ecclesial documents (or indeed theological reflections) to have almost as many references to the Holy Spirit as to Christ.

The faith conviction that the Spirit is actively and foundationally involved in the church is crucially important for synodality, for it lays the basis for a dynamic, living understanding of the church and the Catholic tradition. God has in the past spoken through Christ, and God is still speaking to us now through the Holy Spirit. He does so through the faith intuitions of the people around us, the signs of the times, and the dialogue that we have amongst ourselves and in which we share these intuitions.

That makes synodality much more than a clever strategy to make lay people feel involved or a semi-scientific survey of the *vox populi*; it is a deeply religious, spiritual undertaking to try to heed the Spirit in and through what is being said and what is going on. It made sense, therefore, to start the October 2023 gathering of the synod with a short retreat. For the same

---

31. For the references to the Holy Spirit, see nos. 2 (5 times), 5, 7, 9 (2), 11, 13 (3), 14 (2), 15 (3), 16 (5), 17, 19, 20, 23, 24 (2), 26 (2), 27, 30. There are 2 references to Christ, plus 12 references to Lord (most of which refer to Christ), plus 21 references to Jesus (2 of which are combined with Lord).

32. For the references to the Holy Spirit, see Introduction (3 times), 1c, 1e, 1h, 2a (2), 2d (4), 2f, 2h, 2i, 2j, 2l, 3c (2), 3d, 3e, 3f, 3h, 3i, 4d, 5f, 8a, 8b, 8f, 9b, 9e, 10a, 10b (2), 12b, 14e, 15a, 16c (2), 17c, 19a, 20a, Conclusion (2); in seven cases, the reference is part of the expression "conversation in the Spirit." There are 25 references to Christ, plus 17 references to Lord (most of which mean Christ), plus 28 references to Jesus (6 of which are combined with Christ).

reason, it was very fitting to include moments of silence in the conversation process; avoiding the "echo chamber" in which one only hears oneself, mutual listening can become a space of listening to the Spirit.[33]

This pneumatological focus is one more example of a theological reconfiguration or shift. Obviously, highlighting the Spirit's importance and agency is fully Catholic. Doesn't the Creed confess the Spirit as "the Lord, the giver of life," that is, on an equal footing with the Father and the Son—*Dominum* —with a particular salvation-historical role—*vivificantem?* At the same time, speaking more about the Spirit and wanting to actually listen to the Spirit, as a synodal approach does, means renewal, as giving priority to the Spirit alongside the Father and the Son has not been, nor even is today, a feature of most of theology and church teaching.

A Different Style

One of the reasons that synodality is so distinctive, and sometimes hard to describe, is that its goals are not primarily realized in a series of succinct teachings, that is, in *what* the church teaches, but in the way of proceeding that it promotes, or *how* the church operates. In other words, synodality is not only characterized by faith convictions such as those outlined above but also by a *style*. Pope Francis explicitly refers to style as an important aspect. For example, on the eve of the Synod 2021–24 process, Francis invited the faithful of the Diocese of Rome to be open-minded rather than to stick to the past and the familiar, underlining that "that's the style of our journey" (*questo è lo stile del nostro cammino*).[34] In recent books

33. For the importance of silence, see the explanation in the *Instrumentum Laboris* 2023, 32–42.

34. Pope Francis, Address to the Faithful of the Diocese of Rome. (Unfortunately, the official English translation failed to express the pope's use of the word *style*: "This is how our own journey should be.") For a reflection

on synodality, Latin American theologian Rafael Luciani speaks of "a new way of proceeding," and Italian theologian Serena Noceti subtitled her book *A Synodal Way of Proceeding*.[35]

Concerning style, the Second Vatican Council serves as an example and inspiration, as it distinguished itself from earlier councils precisely in this regard. Throughout Christian history, councils and synods typically gathered to respond—to borrow a popular phrase from American jurisprudence—to a "clear and present danger." The earliest councils and synods took their model from the Roman Senate, which governed by formulating legislation that proscribed or prescribed certain behaviors and established penalties for nonobservance. Following this example, synods and councils gathered to put a stop to ideas and practices that endangered the faith and well-being of the church. Typically, the outcome of synods were short documents that stated which faith convictions or practices were right and which were wrong, with a focus on issuing legislation. They regulated what John O'Malley calls observable behavior: "Even doctrinal decrees were . . . often formulated in canons, and therefore were laws. As laws they dealt with observable behavior, not with motivation or conscience: 'If anyone should *say* such and such—or *teach* or *preach* such and such—let him be anathema,' not 'If anyone should *believe* or *think* such and such.' "[36]

---

on Pope Francis and style, see Christoph Theobald, SJ, "Le christianisme comme style: Mise en perspective de la 'theologies' du pape François," in Theobald, *Le courage de penser l'avenir: Études œcuméniques de theologies fondamentale et ecclésiologique* (Paris: Cerf, 2021), 169–96.

35. Rafael Luciani, *Synodality: A New Way of Proceeding in the Church* (New York: Paulist Press, 2022). Serena Noceti, *Reforming the Church: A Synodal Way of Proceeding* (New York: Paulist Press, 2023).

36. See John O'Malley, SJ, *When Bishops Meet: An Essay Comparing Trent, Vatican I, and Vatican II* (Cambridge: Harvard University Press, 2019), 17. For a more developed reflection, see John O'Malley, SJ, "Vatican II: Did Anything Happen?," *Theological Studies* 67/1 (2006): 3–33.

The Second Vatican Council distinguished itself clearly from these councils. For a start, the council documents are much longer than those of any other council. O'Malley observes, "Vatican II issued 16 final documents. The pagination of these 16 is almost twice the length of the decrees of Trent, and the decrees of Trent and Vatican II together equal in volume the decrees of all the other 19 councils taken together."[37] In the second place, the style of the documents is remarkably different. This council did not issue any condemnation and, instead of setting boundaries, it developed a narrative that was meant to inspire and attract in a "pastoral" style.[38]

Pastoral became a key word for how the council wanted to speak. Pope John XXIII had mentioned the word in his opening address *Gaudet Mater Ecclesia*. By *pastoral*, he meant a way of speaking that is understandable for contemporaries, being rooted in an awareness of the concrete lives of the faithful. (Pope Francis's image comes to mind: pastors should have the smell of the sheep.) While stressing that church teaching was fundamentally unchangeable, the pope also referred to modern context and called for another type of magisterial teaching, more focused on explaining than on condemning, and with "pastoral" features. In his own words: "Types of presentation must be introduced which are more in accord with a teaching authority which is primarily pastoral in character. . . . At the present time, the spouse of Christ prefers to use the medicine of mercy rather than the weapons of severity; and, she thinks she meets today's needs by explaining the validity of her doctrine more fully rather than by condemning."[39]

37. O'Malley, "Vatican II: Did Anything Happen?," 10.
38. Two decades ago, John O'Malley observed that the shift in conciliar form had received less attention than shifts in content, something that has been changing since. See O'Malley, "Vatican II: Did Anything Happen?," 17.
39. Komonchak, "*Gaudet Mater Ecclesia.*"

In the course of the council, the council fathers embraced this notion of *pastoralità* and criticized draft texts that lacked the pastoral spirit of John XXIII. As a result, the texts underwent dramatic changes, which required a lot of work, so that the council needed no less than four annual sessions. But it worked. Although the council was far from a unified body, there is a certain stylistic coherence. The opening sections of *Lumen Gentium* and *Gaudium et Spes* are cases in point. Instead of deploring the evils of the world, the church presents itself in LG 1 and GS 1 as a travel companion who empathizes with the world's joys and sufferings, shares in them, and seeks to share Christ's light. Instead of distancing itself, condemning, or lamenting, the church wants to pass on God's light as a source of comfort—and humbly so, for it first receives what it then passes on.

John O'Malley summarizes the new approach somewhat euphorically when he writes: "From commands to invitations, from laws to ideals, from threats to persuasion, from coercion to conscience, from monologue to conversation, from ruling to serving, from withdrawn to integrated, from vertical and top-down to horizontal, from exclusion to inclusion, from hostility to friendship, from static to changing, from passive acceptance to active engagement, from prescriptive to principled, from defined to open-ended, from behavior-modification to conversion of heart, from the dictates of law to the dictates of conscience, from external conformity to the joyful pursuit of holiness."[40]

The dialogical spirit that one finds in the final texts also marked the council itself. Here, too, Pope John XXIII set the tone when, prior to the council, the global episcopate and a couple of specific groups, such as religious orders and congregations, were consulted in order to identify topics for the

---

40. O'Malley, "Vatican II: Did Anything Happen?," 29–30.

conciliar agenda. Cardinal Domenico Tardini, president of the council's Antepreparatory Commission, proposed distributing a limited questionnaire to the council fathers so that his commission might more easily process the voluminous responses expected—a work that would take several years, he thought. Pope John opted for another approach, rejecting both the questionnaire and the request for a multiple-year preparatory process. Instead, he opted for open consultation and a short preparation. He wanted that the council's work would not be done in advance by members of the Roman Curia, with the world's bishops coming to rubber stamp or, at most, tweak preexisting documents. A strong example of the bishops taking ownership of the council is the fact that they rejected almost all *schemata* (draft texts) that had been prepared in advance. The new drafts took into account what had been said in the council hall.[41]

Highlighting ecclesial style, in fact, builds on a very traditional axiom that faith content (or *fides quae*) and faith attitudes and practices (or *fides qua*) are interconnected. A person who believes that God is an exacting, severe keeper of divine laws will likely develop a fearful and scrupulous faith practice. Conversely, a fearful and scrupulous faith practice is probably grounded in the faith conviction that God is an exacting, severe keeper of divine laws. That also holds true for synodality. Other ways of imagining the People of God in relation to the hierarchy, the church in relation to time, and the Holy Spirit as the church's ultimate guide should translate into other ecclesial styles. For example, the priority of baptism implies a complementary culture of appreciating one another's gifts.

---

41. For a detailed academic historical-genetical account of the council, see Giuseppe Alberigo and Joseph Komonchak, eds., *History of Vatican II*, 5 vols. (Maryknoll, NY: Orbis, 1995–2003). For a running narrative, see John W. O'Malley, *What Happened at Vatican II* (Cambridge: Harvard University Press, 2008).

A journeying church calls for flexibility, and if we believe in the Spirit as protagonist, we should develop attitudes and practices of listening and discerning. Thus, theological and ecclesiological shifts come with shifts in ecclesial practice.

Ultimately, the importance of style takes the focus away from a narrow interest in content only. Synodality is not primarily about solving issues. It is about being on a journey together, with a respectful eagerness to know what other people think and with a spiritual curiosity as to what God might be saying through that.

The Church as a Sacrament of God's Closeness

Finally, synodality is essentially missionary. Communal and participative discernment of what the Spirit is telling the church ultimately concerns her mission. As the Synod 2021–24 theme—"Communion, Participation, Mission"—indicates, synodality is not only about how we relate amongst ourselves but also about going out to share with others. In fact, because mission appeared to be at risk of becoming a somewhat secondary topic, below that of the church's internal functions, the order of the three words in the motto were changed in the *Instrumentum Laboris* (working document) for the 2023 synod gathering to "communion, mission, participation." The text argues that communion and mission mutually include one another and that participation only makes sense once that binary is in place.[42]

A missionary view of the church is particularly dear to Pope Francis. As a matter of fact, it was the very core of his short but powerful address to the cardinals prior to the 2013 conclave that elected him pope. In it, Cardinal Bergoglio contrasted two ways of imagining the church: a self-absorbed,

---

42. *Instrumentum Laboris* 2023, 44.

worldly church and an evangelizing, missionary church. He criticized the former, speaking of a "self-referentiality, a sort of theological narcissism" responsible for "the evils that, over time, happen in ecclesial institutions." Instead, he compared the church to the moon, which has no light of its own but receives its light from elsewhere and reflects it. That church "go[es] out to the peripheries, not only geographically, but also the existential peripheries: those of the mystery of sin, those of pain, those of injustice, those of ignorance and religious indifferences, those of intellectual currents, and those of all misery."[43]

The latter view of the church may be called sacramental. In his classic book on models of the church, Avery Dulles explains that the point of the image of the church as sacrament is, first, that it should be a convincing sign of God's grace and, second, that "the Church should become an event of grace as the lives of its members are transformed in hope, in joy, in self-forgetful love, in peace, in patience, and in the other Christlike virtues."[44] In the background resonates *Lumen Gentium*'s description of the church as "in Christ like a sacrament or as a sign and instrument both of a very closely knit union with God and of the unity of the whole human race" (LG 1) and "the universal sacrament of salvation" (LG 48). Just like each of the seven sacraments, the church both makes God's grace visible ("sign") and mediates and realizes that grace ("instrument").

---

43. After the address, Cardinal Jaime Ortega asked for the text. Jorge Bergoglio handed him some notes he wrote afterwards, which Cardinal Ortega shared with the wider public. The address can be found in various places, for example, Jaime Ortega y Alamino, "Aparecida y Evangelii Gaudium en esta hora de la Iglesia," *Revista Investigación y Pensamiento Crítico* 2/5 (September–December 2014): 99–108, at 104–5. For an English translation, see Gerard O'Connell, *The Election of Pope Francis: An Inside Account of the Conclave That Changed History* (Maryknoll, NY: Orbis, 2019), 153–54.

44. Dulles, *Models of the Church*, 60–63.

This view of the church includes the visible element that was celebrated in the institutional model of the church, which focused on observable things such as a shared creed and a hierarchical structure. Yet it combines the visible element with the transcendent dimension that was celebrated in the Mystical Body model, which imagined the church as Christ's Body.[45] In so doing, it strives to make the visible part of a transcendent dynamic of salvation. A major benefit of understanding the church as sacrament is that it is outgoing; it thus leaves behind more introverted perspectives that are concerned about the inner life of the church itself, such as the church as an institution or even the church as the People of God. The sacramental image foregrounds the dynamic of sharing and passing on.

While the image of church as sacrament was not very prominent during the council, the underlying conviction that it needs to engage constructively with the world was.[46] That conviction marked both the beginning of the council and its conclusion. The first document to be approved was the so-called "Message to Humanity" that the council fathers released on October 20, 1962, just a couple of days after it had started. It was a "message of salvation, love, and peace," addressed to all people and nations. The council said that the church wanted to renew itself so that the Gospel would be understandable in this day and age, that it wanted to serve

45. In fact, there were various versions of Mystical Body theology, with the official one (expressed in Pope Pius XII's 1943 encyclical, *Mystici Corporis*) focusing on the institutional dimension and other ones rather focusing on Christ and the transcendent dimension of the church. For an introduction, see Edward Hahnenberg, "The Mystical Body of Christ and Communion Ecclesiology: Historical Parallels," *Irish Theological Quarterly* 70 (2005): 3–30.

46. See Jan-Heiner Tück, "Sakrament des Heils für die Welt: Annäherungen an einen ekklesiologischen Leitbegriff des Konzils," in *Die großen Metaphern des Zweiten Vatikanischen Konzils: Ihre Bedeutung für heute*, ed. Mariano Delgado and Michael Sievernich, SJ (Freiburg: Herder, 2013), 141–67.

and not to dominate, and that it felt sympathy with the suffering, longing, and hope of all peoples. In particularly, it meant to promote peace, brotherhood, and social justice.[47]

The council ended with the promulgation of a major document that adopted and greatly developed the same stance, the Pastoral Constitution on the Church in the World, *Gaudium et Spes*. The title itself is already meaningful: the church is situated in the world; world and church are not two different realms. The council fathers positioned the church as a fellow traveler who has knowledge of and sympathy for what is going on, before preaching its message. The opening words speak volumes: "The joys and hopes, the grief and anguish of the people of our time, especially of those who are poor or afflicted, are the joys and hopes, the griefs and anguish of the followers of Christ as well. Nothing that is genuinely human fails to find an echo in their hearts" (GS 1). Both documents demonstrate a strong desire to share the Gospel and to pass on God's grace, as the church always had, yet now that desire is rooted in sympathy for the world rather than rejection of it.

Theoretically speaking, synodality has a similar desire that the church be a fellow traveler who shares and passes on. Official synod documents highlight the importance of mission and want to avoid an inward focus on issues of the church, which probably has to do with Francis's fear of an introspective, self-referential church. While theoretically it makes great theological sense to highlight the church as a missionary, sacramental body, it seems, in fact, that *ad intra* issues take up most of the attention in the synodal journey, and that that is right. For synodality to go forward, we need to work on including women, to rethink the role of the ordained in the church, and to develop new habits of decision-making and decision-taking. Making progress

---

47. For the text, see "Message to Humanity," in Walter Abbott, SJ, ed., *The Documents of Vatican II* (New York: Guild Press, 1966), 3–7. Several collections of the council documents do not include the "Message to Humanity."

with these *ad intra* issues is missionary by implication, as it frees new energy and opens new ways of proceeding, both of which serve our mission. Therefore, we should not worry too much about *ad intra* conversations.

Moreover, a synodal way of functioning *ad intra* can be a prophetic sign for a world that is divided and polarized, and it is indeed sometimes presented as such. For example, the working document for the 2023 synod gathering commented that "a synodal Church can offer a prophetic witness to a fragmented and polarised world, especially when its members are committed to walking together with others for the building of the common good." This it also presented as a question: "Is the Christian community able to bear witness to the possibility of concord beyond political polarization?"[48]

Conclusion

So why is synodality a good idea? In the first place, by promoting dialogical practices, synodality acknowledges baptism as the church's foundational sacrament. Sharing the fundamental dignity of having been clothed with Christ and anointed by the Spirit, we may all speak words of wisdom. Dialogue is a means to be enriched by sharing one another's faith intuitions. In the second place, synodality acknowledges the church's situatedness in time, and thus embraces its dynamic nature. Theologically speaking, the church is called to think how best to understand and communicate the faith here and now. Thirdly, the Holy Spirit's guidance and what Pope Francis calls his "protagonist" role invites the church to a great faith that is lived out in a synodal quest for what the Spirit is saying to the church here and now. Fourthly, synodality is characterized by a certain way of proceeding that recalls the

---

48. *Instrumentum Laboris* 2023, section B 1.1, section d and question 5.

distinctive dialogical, fraternal style of the council documents. Finally, we saw that synodality is essentially missionary in nature, which was a key concern of the council also. Thus, the chapter has provided some theological foundations that explain why a listening, journeying church is a good idea; in those foundations, the Second Vatican Council plays a major role.

This chapter has not treated all aspects of synodality. The topic of regional diversity is emerging, leading to the question of how much liturgical, pastoral, or even doctrinal difference the Catholic Church can bear or should embrace.[49] The council's notion of the local church could help develop this further. Another aspect that has emerged is how to "synodalize" parish life, which requires another style of priesthood. Post-conciliar theological reflection on the difference between a cultic priesthood apart from the people and a ministerial priesthood at the service of the community deserves further reception in magisterial thinking. Other big issues are the relationship between revelation and truth, and the role of women. These are all important matters, but they cannot be dealt with here.

---

49. For example, the Synod 2023 left addressing the issue of polygamy to the African bishops. See Synthesis Report 2023, 16q.

Chapter Two

How Did Synodality Emerge?

Historical Considerations

In the previous chapter we described the theological foundations of synodality in general and the synodal process of 2021–24 in particular. Pope Francis stresses the importance of synodality, qualifying it as something "which God expects of the Church of the third millennium" and as "a constitutive element of the Church."[1] Statements like these imply that synodality belongs to the very core of what it means to be Catholic. While some aspects of Catholic faith life, such as particular styles of prayer, may be a matter of individual preference or choice, synodality is essential. This chapter explores what has led to this conviction. How did synodality emerge? How did we get here?

The answer to that question is somewhat tricky. The synodal renewal as we know it would have been impossible without Pope Francis. His choice for synodality can be traced back to his personal spiritual journey from an authoritarian leader to someone who favors consultation, dialogue, and participation, and further relates to his experience in the Latin American

1. Pope Francis, Ceremony Commemorating the 50th Anniversary.

church. While historically one cannot deny the crucial role that Pope Francis has played, the disadvantage of focusing on him is that synodality can easily be dismissed as his personal taste. Can another pope have another preference?

To show that synodality has broader historical roots than Pope Francis, we therefore first discuss two other roots. As Catholic renewal usually draws on history—*aggiornamento* and *ressourcement* go hand-in-hand—we start with rereading early Christian history as described in the Acts of the Apostles. Moreover, as Catholic renewal usually responds to the situation of the contemporary church and the signs of the times, we also dwell on the worldwide sexual abuse crisis, the financial scandals in the Vatican, frustration over excessive centralization, and clerical power games. These developments have matured into the clear conviction that something needs to change in the church. After delving into the Acts of the Apostles and contemporary developments, we conclude the chapter with Pope Francis, who has prophetically noticed that synodality is the change we need.

Biblical Foundations: The Acts of the Apostles

Official documents and theological literature on synodality often refer to the Acts of the Apostles. At the beginning of the Synod 2021–24, Pope Francis highlighted the book as "the first and most important 'manual' of ecclesiology." According to him, the book illustrates that synodality is essential for the church, and not just "a fad or a slogan to be bandied about in our meetings."[2] While Catholics must hold Scripture in great esteem and always have recourse to it as a privileged way through which God speaks to us, we also have to acknowledge that our questions are often different from those that Scrip-

---

2. Pope Francis, Address to the Faithful of the Diocese of Rome.

ture deals with. For example, the New Testament came into being in a context in which the word *synodality* didn't exist and in a culture in which participation and inclusion were certainly *not* key values. So how can it be a handbook for ecclesiology now? Reflecting on synodality, Protestant theologian Céline Rohmer challenges us that we should not turn to Scripture to legitimize what we do, think, and organize, but rather to criticize and question it.[3] After letting go of the illusion that Scripture is a hidden store with all the answers to all the questions for all times, however, Scripture can help us to find orientation.

For a start, we find that life was as challenging for the early Christian community as it is for us now. Arguably, the Acts of the Apostles romanticizes reality when it speaks of Christians harmoniously living together, sharing everything, praising God, growing in numbers, and so on.[4] In fact, the challenges that tried the early Christians were many. Jesus's death shattered the dream of a new kingdom. His resurrection and the outpouring of the Holy Spirit helped to overcome that disillusion, but disappointments remained. Among these was the disappointment that Jesus did not return quickly, as he seemed to have promised. Christians needed to come to grips with the

---

3. Céline Rohmer, "De la tradition synodale à l'événement synodal: ou comment la Bible interroge la pratique," *Recherches de Science Religieuse* 107 (2019): 209–24. Rohmer writes, "The biblical text is not called upon to confirm but to challenge, criticize, and if necessary reform what human traditions establish and end up treating as law" (our translation).

4. See, for example, Acts 2:43-47: "Awe came upon everyone, because many wonders and signs were being done by the apostles. All who believed were together and had all things in common; they would sell their possessions and goods and distribute the proceeds to all, as any had need. Day by day, as they spent much time together in the temple, they broke bread at home and ate their food with glad and generous hearts, praising God and having the goodwill of all the people. And day by day the Lord added to their number those who were being saved."

fact that this so-called *parousia* was apparently not happening any time soon and they needed to embrace life here and now. Other major challenges stemmed from the tensions between rich and poor in the community and the equally divisive rivalry between the various divine gifts (or charisms). These meant that Paul needed all his rhetorical skill to restore communion (see 1 Cor 12–14). And finally, faith was oftentimes lukewarm: all talk but little action (see James).

Reflections on how to be a synodal church often recall yet another crisis. When Christianity started spreading into what are now Greece and Turkey, the question of how to respond to the new context arose. Until that moment, Christianity had been a variant of the Jewish religion; those who became Christians had all been circumcised and observed (more or less) Jewish law. Did new believers in the new territories, in which the Jewish religion was not the norm, have to follow the same practices? Chapters ten to fifteen of the Acts of the Apostles describe in great detail how the drama unfolded. We will briefly recall the story here and then underline various aspects that can inspire a synodal way of proceeding.

It starts in chapter ten with God working hard to teach Peter. To achieve this, God employs a series of instruments: a vision with a voice promoting eating unclean animals, a delegation from the gentile centurion Cornelius, Peter visiting Cornelius in spite of the Jewish law forbidding that, and the Spirit coming down on the (non-Jewish) people while Peter was preaching the Gospel to them. The chapter ends with Cornelius and his friends being baptized: "While Peter was still speaking, the Holy Spirit fell upon all who heard the word. The circumcised believers who had come with Peter were astounded that the gift of the Holy Spirit had been poured out even on the gentiles, for they heard them speaking in tongues and extolling God. Then Peter said, 'Can anyone withhold the water for baptizing these people who have received the Holy Spirit just as we have?' So he ordered them to be baptized in the name of Jesus Christ" (Acts 10:44-48a).

The chapter makes it very clear that Peter oversteps boundaries. It also reveals that God does not demand that the gentiles avoid "unclean" food and that he chooses to pour out the Spirit over the gentiles present at Peter's address; moreover, earlier God had already deigned to speak to the gentile Cornelius in a dream, just as he had to Peter. Seemingly, therefore, God does not demand circumcision.

Understandably, this causes all sorts of rumors and tensions. That is very clear in the opening words of chapter eleven: "Now the apostles and the brothers and sisters who were in Judea heard that the Gentiles had also accepted the word of God. So when Peter went up to Jerusalem, the circumcised believers criticized him, saying, 'Why did you go to uncircumcised men and eat with them?'" (vv. 1-3). Peter then explains to the circumcised believers what had happened, which they find convincing, yet when a new round of complaints reaches Jerusalem, it turns out that the issue has not been resolved, for a new investigation is started. Decisive are the fruits that are visible. For after the church in Jerusalem has sent out Barnabas to explore what's going on, Acts notes: "When he came and saw the grace of God, he rejoiced, and he exhorted them all to remain faithful to the Lord with steadfast devotion; for he was a good man, full of the Holy Spirit and of faith. And a great many people were brought to the Lord" (vv. 23-24).

The same issue surfaces again at the beginning of chapter fifteen, this time with Paul and Barnabas as the main characters. Chapter thirteen describes how Barnabas and Paul have been sent out by the church in Antioch. Even though most of the missionary work is with Jews and in synagogues, non-Jews listened to them, too, "and as many as had been destined for eternal life became believers" (Acts 13:48b). This happens in various places (see Acts 14) and stirs up a fierce discussion between those of the old persuasion—one should be a Jew to become a Christian—and Paul and Barnabas. Ultimately, this leads to a meeting with "much debate" (Acts 15:6) among all the main leaders in Jerusalem, which includes witnesses of what happened, an interpretation of events in light of Scripture, and a decision by James, after which a letter is sent out on what "the Holy Spirit and we" have decided (Acts 15:6-29).

In this story of the so-called Council of Jerusalem, we can recognize elements of what we today call synodality. What light does this story shed on synodality?

1. New questions may arise. Synodality is not afraid of facing new questions.

2. While seeking to respond to these new questions, openness to God's action is crucial. The story suggests that God may act in a variety of ways, such as—in this case— a vision with angels (Cornelius), a trance with a vision and a voice (Peter), non-Jews such as Cornelius who act as instruments, and so on. Synodality is a faith process that is open to what Pope Francis calls "the surprises of the Spirit."

3. God does not operate the same way in each person at the same time, which often leads to different perspectives at different times and, therefore, to conflicts. Synodality is not afraid of difference and conflict.

4. Decisive for the process are patient listening to one another, generous openness to God, and confident trust in the process. Synodality presupposes a commitment to fraternal communion and is willing to invest time and energy in that.

5. Finally, the process leads to new conclusions, based on a rereading of the Scriptures. At various instances in the story, protagonists recount the "traditional" faith understanding in a new way. Peter does so in the house of Cornelius (chapter ten), when he is with the Christians in Jerusalem (chapter eleven), and when he is among the apostles and elders in Jerusalem (chapter fifteen). The decisive speech by James is based on a rereading of

Amos (chapter fifteen). Importantly, all (or, more realistically, most) agree with the new perspective. Synodality may lead to new outcomes.

Chapters ten through fifteen of the Acts of the Apostles are by no means the only biblical references that shed light on what synodality is. The story of the disciples on the way to Emmaus in Luke 24 powerfully illustrates how human conversations may become a place of encounter with God. The promise of "another Advocate . . . the Spirit of truth" in John 14:16-17 encourages us to be open to God speaking to us here and now. So, too, does the emphasis on "listen[ing] to what the Spirit is saying to the churches" in Revelation 2 that Pope Francis particularly likes. One may also point to passages such as 1 Corinthians 12–14, on how to live well as a community.[5]

Signs of the Times: Crises That Call for Synodality

The events detailed in the Acts of the Apostles happened a long time ago. But what makes what happened *then* meaningful for *our* time and context, which are so different? What makes synodality worthwhile *now*? In this section, we will explore several recent developments in the church and society that call for synodality. While synodality grows out of the theological considerations described in the first chapter, it also emerged as a response to these developments. They include various crises affecting the church, such as sexual abuse, financial scandals in the Vatican, and clerical abuses of power. Spiritually and theologically speaking, God can even act in and speak through crises. As our experience tells us and as

5. See the "Biblical Resources for Synodality," published online by the synod's Commission on Spirituality (2022), https://www.synod.va/content/dam/synod/common/spirituality/Biblical-Resouces-for-Synodality-A4-EN.pdf. It also highlights Psalm 107, Joshua 24, Nehemiah 8:1-12, Acts 1:13-14, Acts 10:1–11:18, Acts 15:1-35, and Ephesians 4.

Scripture testifies, crises can be times of conversion; they can be a *kairos*, a time of grace. In one of his talks at the retreat that preceded the October 2023 synodal meetings, Dominican friar Timothy Radcliffe commented that his Dominican brethren had become so accustomed to hearing him say that a crisis can be a time of grace that they gave him a t-shirt that said, "Have a good crisis!"[6] Moreover, theology reminds us that the signs of the times—events around us, in world and church—can speak about God and shed light on the Gospel. In this section we will first list a few recent and ongoing crises and then suggest how synodality may be an appropriate way to respond to them.

The first of these is the abuse crisis that has been unfolding since the 1980s, with one watershed moment being the infamous 2002 revelations by *The Boston Globe* (dramatized in the 2015 movie *Spotlight*). It became clear then that the problem was much larger than isolated cases, such as that of Fr. Marcial Maciel, the founder of the Legionaries of Christ, who had abused seminarians and had a lover and a daughter, and who was suspended from ministry in 2006—abuse and cover-up were everywhere. In many dioceses and religious congregations, it had been standard practice to transfer abusive priests to another parish or diocese and to simply cover up abuse rather than to listen to the victims.

Vatican affairs journalist Gerard O'Connell recalls that the abuse crisis was very present indeed in the minds of the cardinals at the 2013 conclave: "It hovered like a dark cloud over their pre-conclave meetings as organizations representing victims of abuse . . . called on several cardinals not to participate in the election because of their alleged failure to have dealt properly with abuse cases in their dioceses."[7] The crisis came

---

6. Timothy Radcliffe, OP, *Listening Together: Meditations on Synodality* (Collegeville, MN: Liturgical Press, 2024), 105.

7. O'Connell, *Election of Pope Francis*, xx.

particularly close when, just prior to the conclave, the Scottish cardinal Keith O'Brien resigned because of revelations of "unbecoming conduct," as he put it himself, upon which he decided not to take part in the conclave.[8]

The abuse crisis has continued under Pope Francis. Austen Ivereigh singles out the *"annus horribilis"* 2018, which included devastating revelations in Australia, Germany, and the United States, the Theodore McCarrick case, the Pope's most unfortunate visit to Chile and the disastrous investigation that followed,[9] and the Carlo Maria Viganò saga.[10] It has manifested itself more recently in the high-profile case of Jean Vanier, the founder of L'Arche, whose abusive relationships with women in the context of spiritual accompaniment were established in a nine-hundred-page report published in January 2023. It also continues to manifest itself at the level of dioceses, religious congregations, and countries, some of which have already faced their past, with others still hoping—usually in vain—that there was no abuse and no cover up in their country, congregation, or continent.

Another crisis that has highlighted the need for synodality is the way Rome relates to other parts of the ecclesial world. On the one hand, the church is becoming more and more a global, non-Western church. This would suggest decentralization and inculturation, so as to respect local, non-Western realities.[11] On the other hand, the church's governance in the post-conciliar era has been characterized by centralizing tendencies that are

8. O'Connell, *Election of Pope Francis*, 67–68. The resignation was on February 25, 2013. The first day of the pre-conclave gatherings was on March 4, with the conclave proper starting on March 12.

9. See Sandra Arenas, "The Awakening of Chile: Demands for Participation and the Synodal Church," *Louvain Studies* 45 (2022): 97–111.

10. Austen Ivereigh, *Wounded Shepherd: Pope Francis and His Struggle to Convert the Catholic Church* (New York: Henry Holt, 2019), 100–148.

11. See Massimo Faggioli, *The Liminal Papacy of Pope Francis: Moving toward Global Catholicism* (Maryknoll, NY: Orbis, 2020).

closely linked with a certain reception of the Second Vatican
Council that typically promotes uniformity rather than diversity
and distrust rather than trust. These two tendencies clashed,
for example, in the case of the new English translation of the
Roman Missal, officially approved in 2010. An earlier retransla-
tion, completed in 1998 by an international group of experts,
had been approved unanimously by eleven Anglophone bishops'
conferences, but the Vatican's Dicastery for Divine Worship
overturned that approval and then went on to produce its own
translation, one that was pastorally, theologically, and estheti-
cally inferior to the 1998 version, as the Australian Jesuit and
longtime Gregorian University professor Gerald O'Collins pain-
fully demonstrated in his book on the matter.[12] The issue at
stake is not only liturgy but also power. The fact that a Vatican
dicastery can and did overrule unanimous local leadership from
a variety of countries and continents speaks of strong centralizing tendencies.

Various other scandals and issues that have erupted from
within the Vatican also demonstrate the importance of synodality in the life of the church, beginning with the so-called
Vatileaks scandal of 2012. About a year prior to the 2013
conclave, the Italian journalist Gianluigi Nuzzi published a
sensational book that unveiled, through leaked documents
taken from the desk of Pope Benedict XVI, a culture of corruption and clerical power games. By the time of the conclave,
the storm had not subsided; indeed, many have theorized that
the Vatileaks scandal played a strong role in Benedict's decision to resign from his office, feeling himself to be no longer
up to its demands. As O'Connell recalls, "Cardinals, especially
those from Europe, the Americas, and Australia who were
more aware of what had happened, were concerned by the

---

12. See Gerald O'Collins, SJ, with John Wilkins, *Lost in Translation: The
English Language and the Catholic Mass* (Collegeville, MN: Liturgical Press,
2017).

leaks, the alleged corruption, the infighting, and much else that had been revealed and that was damaging the Church's credibility. Before electing a new pope, they wanted to understand the real situation in the Vatican and what problems he would have to deal with."[13]

Another scandal that played out during this same period was the increased public awareness of questionable financial dealings of the Vatican bank (officially called the Institute for the Works of Religion, or IOR). The Vatican's finances were so problematic that the Vatican was included on the United Nations' list of "the world's most attractive financial laundromats."[14] Since that time, progress has been made, with greater involvement of financial experts from outside the Vatican and outside Italy. Moreover, the 2023 conviction of Cardinal Becciu for embezzlement (after he had already been stripped of his rights as a cardinal in 2020) indicates the end of impunity, although changing a culture is a long-term project.

An ongoing concern has been the issue of careerism—a tendency among some ordained men to live priestly or episcopal ministry as a career path—and clericalism—a tendency of some of the ordained to place themselves above "the others." Careerism and clericalism deform ministry, making power, not service, central and focusing on oneself, not on the Gospel. Clerical and careerist people feel that they are different from the ordinary faithful by virtue of their ordination, their knowledge, and their connection with God, and they often express this through a lifestyle of luxury and privilege. Pope Francis has used several annual Christmas addresses to the Roman Curia to criticize this, such as his famous 2014

13. O'Connell, *Election of Pope Francis*, xxi. See also what O'Connell writes on the second day of the pre-conclave meetings, at 96 and 125–31. The research report that was concluded in December 2022 was, in fact, not shared with the cardinals.

14. Ivereigh, *Wounded Shepherd*, 53.

address in which he listed fifteen "curial diseases."[15] Instead of cold, distant, haughty, and self-centered clergy, the pope called the ordained to be close to the people, in dialogue with them, and at their service.

The Need for Another Leadership Style

We have listed three major crises: an ongoing global crisis of sexual abuse and its cover-up, the Curia's centralizing tendency and power politics, and a set of scandals within the Vatican relating to clerical culture. To understand how synodality can help to overcome these crises, it is important to take one more step by reflecting on the deeper issue. Is weak leadership the real issue? If so, the way forward would be opting for a strong leader who is up to the task. O'Connell recalls that during the conclave, "many foreign cardinals, but also several Italians, were looking to elect a pope who could govern, clean house, and bring order in the Roman Curia."[16] Austen Ivereigh suggested the same thing in his 2014 biography of Francis with the telling title, *The Great Reformer*.

That answer is not very convincing for various reasons. In the first place, it is not true for Francis. After having spoken with Francis, Ivereigh has come to regret the way he presented the pope in *The Great Reformer*. In the prologue of his subsequent 2019 book on Francis's pontificate, *Wounded Shepherd*, he recalls that, when discussing his earlier biography, "[the Pope] was warning me against the 'great man' myth beloved of Hollywood," which made Ivereigh "realize that *The Great Reformer* contributed to that myth. . . . I cringe now that I even likened

---

15. Pope Francis, Presentation of the Christmas Greetings to the Roman Curia, December 22, 2014, https://www.vatican.va/content/francesco/en/speeches/2014/december/documents/papa-francesco_20141222_curia-romana.html.

16. O'Connell, *Election of Pope Francis*, xi.

him to a gaucho riding out at first light."[17] In the prologue of
the newer book, Ivereigh stresses rather that the pope is not
the great hero who vanquishes all troubles, like the protagonists
in Hollywood movies, but that he should be seen as a wounded
shepherd who struggles to convert the church.

In the second place, strong leaders usually cannot withstand
the temptation to serve not only the good cause but also their
own name, reputation, and financial well-being. That means
that, while strong leadership seems promising, it is, in fact,
conducive to the sort of crises that we have already listed. The
church is no exception. A strong leader will face the temptation to protect his own name or that of the institution that he
belongs to, rather than listening to victims of abuse. The strong
leader will face the temptation to place himself on a pedestal
and grant himself favors. And strong leadership leads to a
"court culture" with people flocking around the leader and
pleasing him in the hope of enjoying some favors also—the
very type of culture exposed in the Vatileaks. And finally,
strong leaders rarely delegate power to others; in other words,
strong leadership usually comes with a centralizing logic.

Another possible answer is that the root of the problem is
clericalism: the self-content culture that was described above,
and in which there is no need to listen. It comes with a culture
of silence. Whatever challenges the status quo or sheds a negative light on those on the pedestal should not be said.[18] If this
is so, the way forward would be the exact opposite, namely,
a way of proceeding without pedestals, without privileges, so
that what needs to be said will be said.

This seems to be Pope Francis's answer. As we have seen
earlier, he encourages speaking out and explicitly targets clericalism. The two go together. For example, at the opening of

---

17. Ivereigh, *Wounded Shepherd*, see his prologue, at 1–3.
18. See Donald Cozzens's troubling book *Sacred Silence: Denial and the
Crisis in the Church* (Collegeville, MN: Liturgical Press, 2004).

the Synod on Young People, the Faith, and Vocational Discernment (2018), he first sang the praises of dialogue, listening, and discernment: "At the beginning of the Synod Assembly, [I wish] to invite everyone to speak with courage and frankness (*parrhesia*), namely to integrate freedom, truth and charity. Only dialogue can help us grow. An honest, transparent critique is constructive and helpful, and does not engage in useless chatter, rumors, conjectures or prejudices. . . . The Synod is an ecclesial exercise in discernment. To speak frankly and listen openly are fundamental if the Synod is to be a process of discernment." Towards the end of the same address, he contrasted this with clericalism, and he did not mince his words: "Clericalism arises from an elitist and exclusivist vision of vocation, that interprets the ministry received as a power to be exercised rather than as a free and generous service to be given. This leads us to believe that we belong to a group that has all the answers and no longer needs to listen or learn anything, or that pretends to listen. Clericalism is a perversion and is the root of many evils in the Church: we must humbly ask forgiveness for this and above all create the conditions so that it is not repeated."[19]

This seems a more convincing way of dealing with the ecclesial crises listed earlier. Inviting outsiders' voices and perspectives breaks open closed group dynamics intended to protect those on the inside from those on the outside. Conversation and dialogue get priority over top-down communications. (We see this reflected in the new approach of Vatican dicasteries to the *Ad Limina* visits of the world's bishops. Officials express an eagerness to listen to the experiences of the bishops, who previously sometimes felt treated "like errant altar boys

19. Pope Francis, Address at the Opening of the Synod of Bishops on Young People, the Faith and Vocational Discernment, October 3, 2018, https://www.vatican.va/content/francesco/en/speeches/2018/october /documents/papa-francesco_20181003_apertura-sinodo.html.

rather than the successors of the apostles."[20]) Questions or objections will not lead to smear campaigns or be conveniently ignored; they become part of a normal process of seeking truth and wisdom. It is not difficult to see how synodality means to do just that.

Obviously, challenges, questions, and objections need discernment. The objective must always be to improve the way the church carries out its mission of promoting the kingdom of God. Crucially, however, in a synodal configuration discernment is not determined by the ecclesial status of whoever happens to be offering a proposal but by the question of what serves or doesn't serve the Gospel; as such, there is a strong egalitarian dimension to synodal discernment. Crucially, too, the focus is on promoting the kingdom of God and the well-being of one's brothers and sisters rather than on one's own status, money, or privileges. Clearly, therefore, a collegial and synodal mindset does not go well with abuse, a cover-up culture, unethical financial practices, sexual hypocrisy, and so on.

In embracing a new ecclesial leadership style, secular developments play a role, too. In the course of the twentieth century, democracy became the dominant style of governing in the West, rooted in the dignity and freedom of every human person, as expressed in the Universal Declaration of Human Rights. As we recalled earlier, secular developments can be valued theologically as signs of the times, but official documents on synodality usually do not have a positive take on democracy, stressing rather that synodality is *not* like democracy. While there are certainly differences, it seems difficult to deny that synodality and democracy are part of a general trend in both society and church away from authoritarian and elitist ways of governance, towards equality and participation.

20. See Ivereigh, *Wounded Shepherd*, 77–78.

Polarization and VUCA

Importantly, synodality is also a response to still another crisis that we have not yet mentioned, one that seems to affect the entire globe, namely, the worrying increase of polarization in both church and society, and a simultaneous increase of right-wing political sentiments. Typically, polarization focuses on differences between groups of people—differences in faith conviction, political viewpoints, sexual orientation, cultural background, and so on—and treats them as walls of separation rather than starting points for encounter. The difference in synodality's approach is striking; a synodal logic also starts with difference but makes it the starting point of encounter, dialogue, and discernment. Thus, a synodal church may bear witness to living unity-in-diversity in quite a different way. As the *Instrumentum Laboris* 2023 notes, "A synodal Church can offer a prophetic witness to a fragmented and polarized world, especially when its members are committed to walking together with others for the building of the common good. In places marked by deep conflict, this requires the ability to be agents of reconciliation and artisans of peace."[21]

The impact of polarization makes a synodal—that is, conversational and relational—attitude all the more important today. Looking at the world in the early decades of the twenty-first century, the variety of challenges—including an escalating climate crisis, toxic political polarization, wars raging across the globe, and countless tragic examples of racial and economic injustice—is baffling.

Academics have tried to capture the character of this destabilizing context with the acronym VUCA, which stands for "volatility, uncertainty, complexity, and ambiguity." It was first developed by experts at the US Army War College in the late

---

21. *Instrumentum Laboris* 2023, 1.1. See also the document's image of the church as "a formative 'gymnasium,'" at 87.

1980s to describe the situation following the collapse of the Soviet Union, when many societies and organizations suffered a "multiple-system failure" in which many of the vital structures and ideas that had long provided order and stability simultaneously broke down. This type of large-scale meltdown occurred within former Soviet bloc countries and, paradoxically, also in countries like the United States, for which the loss of an adversary that had shaped its self-understanding, agenda, and worldview triggered something of an identity crisis. VUCA was developed to describe this new climate in the hope that naming it would help catalyze the development of innovative leadership skills and strategic priorities to navigate it.

VUCA observes that the world today is volatile, in that situations are constantly changing and becoming increasingly unstable; there is a sense that things could erupt at any moment. Further, it is shaped by a tremendous uncertainty arising from a lack of information and an inability to predict how events will unfold. In this uncertain environment, traditional means of forecasting and anticipating events are no longer reliable, and thus planning for the future seems impossible. The world is also tremendously complex, in that problems appear to have countless interconnected parts and variables, making it impossible to identify a clear relationship between causes and effects. Finally, the world as we know it is marked by ambiguity. We face a variety of "unknown unknowns" that leave us with the impression that decision-making involves a high degree of risk and requires a constant readiness to accept failure.

More recently, a new acronym, BANI, has been suggested as a replacement for VUCA by those who feel that, especially in the wake of the COVID-19 pandemic, the latter no longer captures the present reality. BANI stands for "brittle, anxious, nonlinear, and incomprehensible." The word *brittle* points to the fact that organizations, situations, and relationships that appear reliable, flexible, and even sturdy are often deceiving because, in reality, their breaking point lies just beneath the surface. This creates a sense that nothing can be trusted. Importantly, not only are organizations, situations, and relationships brittle, but individuals are also brittle; in the wake of overwhelming and ongoing challenges, they lack the mental and emotional resources to deal with new crises and complexities. The current climate is filled with anxiety as we are bombarded with headlines that fill us with worry and leave us waiting for the next disaster. The world today is nonlinear and incomprehensible in that the unpredictable character of events seems to defy any kind of logic. This inability to comprehend situations seems to result not from a lack of information, but from the fact that the information and data we receive is overwhelming.

Regardless of whether BANI or VUCA is more fitting to describe the contemporary reality, it is clear that we live in complex times that frustrate efforts to build community and find a fruitful path into the future. If we look around us for models of how to navigate this unstable context, we see political and religious leaders who proffer solutions that involve drawing lines of social, political, and ethnic demarcation. Here synodality offers a strikingly different model, focusing on encounter, dialogue, relation, discernment.

Importantly, according to Pope Francis, resolving the crises discussed so far requires more than a change in the way we deal with things within the church. For Francis, the church needs to recall her missionary calling of proclaiming and mediating God's closeness and mercy. He is particularly adamant that the church should not be self-centered and inward-focused. There is a need to shift her focus from power to service. Here, too, synodality can be part of the solution, but on one condition: it should be not only about communion and participation but also about mission.

The issue of a church mediating God's *cercanía*—that is, closeness to the people—has come up repeatedly in Francis's teaching and preaching. In fact, it dates back to his time as rector of the Colegio Maximo, the Jesuit seminary in the San Miguel region of Buenos Aires. It was also prominent in Francis's pre-conclave address to his fellow cardinals on the state of the church and what it needs. In that talk, taking up the theme of evangelization that others had spoken about and recalling Paul VI's expression "the sweet and comforting joy of evangelizing," Francis spoke about apostolic zeal and about going out to the frontiers to serve those who suffer—the poor, the needy, the sinners. He also spoke about a self-absorbed church that—by being self-centered—stops passing on God's light. All this can be read as a barely veiled critique of the state of the church at the time of the 2013 conclave. It also explains the direction in which he has led the church under his watch: it should be close to the people, and ministers should be servants of salvation.[22]

In hindsight, one can recognize in this 2013 address a description of Pope Francis's own ministry. While he himself is arguably a strong character and a strong leader, the focus of his leadership is rather to accompany the church in a transformation process in the direction he calls pastoral conversion. The point of the church, its ministers as well as the faithful, should be *cercanía*, closeness to the people. This contrasts sharply with the concern that characterized the sexual abuse crisis, the various scandals in the Vatican, and the Curia's centralizing politics.

Moreover, it is a response to a crisis that we have not mentioned so far, namely, the crisis of faith. Interestingly, that crisis takes different forms in different places. While the West struggles with secularization, Latin America does so with the attraction of the prosperity gospel. The main issue in Asia is that of being a minority in a sometimes-intolerant social context, which makes interreligious dialogue of the highest importance. For Francis, these crises,

22. See chap. 1, note 43.

and those of wars, poverty and refugees, essentially call the church to be present and to accompany:[23] "Closeness: that's the program."[24] Being close to people means not only carrying the smell of the sheep but also listening to the concerns of the people—which brings us back to synodality.

Pope Francis and the Experience of Latin America

The foregoing considerations have already touched on Pope Francis's role in promoting synodality, which we will elaborate in greater detail now. Francis has spoken about synodality from the very start of his pontificate. In a memorable 2015 address, he said that "from the beginning of my ministry as Bishop of Rome, I sought to enhance the Synod."[25] One finds him doing so in interviews, such as his notable 2013 interview with Antonio Spadaro, editor of the Jesuit journal *La Civiltà Cattolica*, shortly after his election,[26] or the 2020 interview by the British journalist Austen Ivereigh that was published as the book *Let Us Dream: The Path to a Better Future*.

His words have materialized in various actions that speak of a desire to consult and collaborate in a participative and inclusive way. The pope meets three times a year with the "Council of Cardinals"—a small group of cardinals from all over the world also known as the "C9"—to discuss the events in the church. He has appointed various women to key positions in the Vatican, such as the undersecretary of the Synod

---

23. O'Connell, *Election of Pope Francis*, xiii–xxvii.

24. Ivereigh, *Wounded Shepherd*, 161.

25. Pope Francis, Ceremony Commemorating the 50th Anniversary. See also Massimo Faggioli, "From Collegiality to Synodality: Promise and Limits of Francis's 'Listening Primacy,'" *Irish Theological Quarterly* 85 (2020): 352–69.

26. Antonio Spadaro, SJ, "A Big Heart Open to God: An Interview with Pope Francis," *America*, September 30, 2013, https://www.america magazine.org/faith/2013/09/30/big-heart-open-god-interview-pope-francis.

of Bishops (Sr. Nathalie Becquart, 2021) and secretary general of the Governorate of the Vatican City (Sr. Raffaella Petrini, 2021). One Vatican press release spoke of the Synod of Bishops taking on "a processual dimension" that aimed to "foster more mature reflection for the greater good of the Church."[27] Finally, Francis invited lay people, including women, as full participants of the Synod 2021–24, which means that they vote just like bishops do.[28]

Pope Francis's preference for synodality is grounded in his own life experience. In his first major interview as pope, looking back on his stint as a provincial at the young age of thirty-six, Francis admitted his initial tendency towards self-sufficient leadership. He spoke of "my authoritarian way of making decisions" and stated: "I made my decisions abruptly and by myself."[29] After a profound crisis—after a successful spell as a novice master, provincial, and rector of the formation house Colegio Maximo, Jesuit leadership stripped Bergoglio of his responsibilities and sent him first to Germany for a doctorate and then to the countryside town of Córdoba, far away from his followers, friends, and supporters, where Bergoglio felt his life had failed[30]—he decided to do things differently once he had become the Archbishop of Buenos Aires. As he explained in the Spadaro interview: "I had a meeting with the six auxiliary bishops every two weeks, and several times a year with the council of priests. They asked questions and we opened the floor for discussion. This greatly helped me to make the best decisions."

27. See Press Communiqué from the General Secretariat of the Synod, October 16, 2022, synod.va/content/dam/synod/news/2022-10-16 _prolungamento/2022.10.16_Comunicato_EN.pdf.

28. For explanation, see https://www.synod.va/en/news/some-news-for -the-october-2023-assembly.html (April 26, 2023).

29. Spadaro, "Big Heart Open to God."

30. See Austen Ivereigh, *The Great Reformer: Francis and the Making of a Radical Pope* (New York: Henry Holt, 2014), 165–209.

At the very beginning of his pontificate, Francis vowed to continue that practice. In the same Spadaro interview, he stated, "I hear some people tell me: 'Do not consult too much, and decide by yourself.' Instead, I believe that consultation is very important."

However, Francis had also experienced firsthand that church leadership did not usually adopt such a consultative approach. While there is a hint of that awareness in the same interview—Francis speaks of the importance of real, not token, consultations—it is especially clear in his comments prior to the opening of the 2014 Synod on the Family. In those comments, Francis encouraged the participants to speak their mind: "One general and basic condition is this: speaking honestly. Let no one say: 'I cannot say this, they will think this or this of me . . .'. It is necessary to say with *parrhesia* all that one feels." And to dispel any doubt about what he meant, he also shared an anecdote on how a synod should *not* work, namely, being your master's voice.

> After the last Consistory (February 2014), in which the family was discussed, a Cardinal wrote to me, saying: what a shame that several Cardinals did not have the courage to say certain things out of respect for the Pope, perhaps believing that the Pope might think something else. This is not good, this is not synodality, because it is necessary to say all that, in the Lord, one feels the need to say: without polite deference, without hesitation. And, at the same time, one must listen with humility and welcome, with an open heart, what your brothers say. Synodality is exercised with these two approaches.[31]

---

31. Pope Francis, Greeting of Pope Francis to the Synod Fathers during the First General Congregation of the Third Extraordinary General Assembly of the Synod of Bishops, October 6, 2014, https://www.vatican.va /content/francesco/en/speeches/2014/october/documents/papa-francesco _20141006_padri-sinodali.html.

The technical term for this is *parrhesia*: speaking frankly and honestly. The term is typical Francis vocabulary and has been adopted in official documents for the Synod 2021–24. For example, the synod's *Vademecum*, or handbook, included it in its list of attitudes needed for participating in a synod: "Being synodal requires time for sharing: We are invited to speak with authentic courage and honesty (*parrhesia*) in order to integrate freedom, truth, and charity. Everyone can grow in understanding through dialogue."[32] As the quote illustrates, *parrhesia* does not mean acting out or ranting. Rather, it means contributing one's perspective to the conversation, while being ready to take in other contributions, in view of growing together in wisdom. Thus, speaking frankly and listening humbly go together.

For Francis, welcoming diverse and opposed views also has intellectual grounds. In the polarized context of Argentinian politics and theology, Francis became convinced that human thoughts are always unfinished. Famously, he preached in 2014 that "the Jesuit must be a person whose thought is incomplete, in the sense of being engaged in open-ended thinking."[33] Instead of a culture that prizes certainty about even the most prudential matters, Francis promotes a culture of discernment on the basis of a variety of perspectives, with input from conversation with others and from encountering reality. As Massimo Borghesi shows, this stance draws on Bergoglio's study of authors such as Augustine, Erich Przywara, Henri de Lubac, Alberto Methol Ferré, and Romano Guardini, and has a base in politics, spirituality, philosophy, and theology.[34]

---

32. General Secretariat for the Synod, *Vademecum* 2.3.

33. Homily on the Liturgical Memorial of the Most Holy Name of Jesus, January 3, 2014, https://www.vatican.va/content/francesco/en/homilies/2014/documents/papa-francesco_20140103_omelia-santissimo-nome-gesu.html.

34. See Massimo Borghesi, *The Mind of Pope Francis: Jorge Mario Bergoglio's Intellectual Journey*, trans. Barry Hudock (Collegeville, MN: Liturgical Press, 2018), 1–141.

Welcoming diversity and opposing views unavoidably means welcoming tensions, as well. For Bergoglio, these are life-giving, for they open up new perspectives. In a 2016 conversation with Antonio Spadaro, he made clear that he sees such tension as normal: "Opposition opens a path, a way forward. Speaking generally, I have to say that I love opposition. Romano Guardini helped me with his book *Der Gegensatz*, which was important to me. He spoke of a polar opposition in which the two opposites are not annulled. One pole does not destroy the other. . . . For him, opposition is resolved at a higher level. In such a solution, however, the polar tension remains . . .; they are not like contradictions."[35]

Francis believes that when we are stuck in a question or problem that seems to offer no way out, over time our thinking will mature towards solutions at a higher level. If we remain open to new approaches or perspectives, we will be surprised by new insights that help us forward. When these new insights come with a sense of harmony, we know that the Holy Spirit is at work. Francis calls this "overflow": God generously surprises us with a new perspective that "breaks the banks that confined our thinking, and causes to pour forth, as if from an overflowing fountain, the answers that formerly the contraposition didn't let us see."[36]

So, Francis's preference for synodality has to do with his character, his experience of politics in Argentina, and his intellectual formation. His synodal sympathies are also inspired by the strong tradition of the Latin American episcopal conference (CELAM) of journeying together (especially bishops) and relating to the poor. In the years following the Second Vatican Council, the Latin American and Caribbean bishops built a unique tradition of collegiality, with continental general conferences in Medellín (1968), Puebla (1979), Santo Domingo

35. Quoted in Borghesi, *Mind of Pope Francis*, 105.
36. Ivereigh, *Let Us Dream*, 80. See also 82–83, 87–89.

(1992), and Aparecida (2007).[37] Thanks to these meetings, the continent embraced a moderate version of liberation theology and the preferential option for the poor that avoids the cliffs on "the right" of siding with the establishment and ignoring the poor as well as those on "the left" of opting for a Marxist revolution. These ideas stand against the background of a theology of the People of God as an active subject of its own history. The poor are not only there to be served or saved, but they also have something to tell and to teach.[38] Or in terms of the Synod 2021–24: participation and mission go together.

Jorge Bergoglio is fully part of this tradition. As the rector of the Colegio Maximo, he made visits to the poor a standard element of Jesuit formation.[39] For Bergoglio, being close to the poor is part of a *Catholic* response to the social reality of poverty that is so present in the continent. Moreover, Bergoglio participated closely in the continental ecclesial reflection process. Rafael Luciani observes that in 1985, as the rector of the Colegio Maximo, Bergoglio was the first to organize a congress exclusively focused on inculturation. Luciani argues that this was an important step in the reception of the 1979 Puebla Conference, which had highlighted the importance of the concrete, local culture in

37. The first General Conference was in 1955, before the council. There is ample literature on CELAM, especially in Spanish. For a succinct overview in English, see Birgit Weiler, MMS, "Synodality in a Continental Perspective: Latin America and the Caribbean," in *Witnesses of Synodality: Good Practices and Experiences*, ed. Jos Moons, SJ, 131–44 (Mahwah, NJ: Paulist Press, 2024).

38. See Pedro Trigo, SJ, "Synodality with the People: A Latin American Perspective," in *Reforming the Church: Global Perspectives*, ed. Declan Marmion and Salvador Ryan (Collegeville, MN: Liturgical Press, 2023), 113–34. For a similar, European perspective, see Étienne Grieu, SJ, "Les plus pauvres au cœur de l'Église?," in *Les derniers seront les premiers: La parole des pauvres au cœur de la synodalité*, ed. François Odinet (Paris: Éditions de l'Emmanuel, 2022), 32–50.

39. See Ivereigh, *Great Reformer*, 180–84.

which the Gospel needs to incarnate. Afterwards, Vatican documents such as Pope John Paul II's apostolic exhortation *Ecclesia in America* (1999) kept this notion but shifted the focus from the people as a subject from whom we may learn to the individual person and their conversion. In its Latin American understanding, inculturation means that the church needs to go out to meet reality and to learn from the encounter between that reality and the Gospel, but *Ecclesia in America* located the learning and conversion process not predominantly in the church but in the individual.[40]

Bergoglio's involvement in CELAM came to a high point when he was chosen to head the committee drafting the final texts of the Aparecida meeting in 2007. Commentators such as Carlos Maria Galli and Austen Ivereigh underline the importance of Aparecida for understanding Pope Francis. Galli writes, "The novelty of Francis' pontificate is related with the newness of Aparecida. Yesterday, Bergoglio gave us Aparecida; today, Aparecida gives us Francis."[41] While that assessment might be marked as much by devotional enthusiasm as by factual truth, it is certainly helpful to see that Aparecida stands for a style, a way of proceeding, with pastoral closeness being at the center. In talking about the importance of shep-

40. Rafael Luciani, *El Papa Francisco y la teología del pueblo* (Madrid: PPC, 2016), 104–12. See also Borghesi, *Mind of Pope Francis*, 44–55.

41. Quoted in Austen Ivereigh, "Hearing the Spirit in the Assembly of the People: Pope Francis's Vision of Synodality," *Studium: Rivista bimestrale di cultura* 117 (2021): 360. For the original, see Carlos Maria Galli, "Revolución de la ternura y reforma de la iglesia," in *Reforma de estructuras y conversión de mentalidades: Retos y desafíos para una Iglesia Sinodal*, ed. Rafael Luciani and Carlos Federico Schickendantz (Madrid: Khaf, 2020), 84. "Ayer Bergoglio contribuyó con Aparecida; hoy Aparecida contribuye con Francisco." See also Diego Fares, SJ, "Ten Years on from Aparecida: The Source of Francis' Pontificate," *La Civiltà Cattolica* (August 14, 2017), https://www.laciviltacattolica.com/ten-years-on-from-aparecida-the-source-of-francis-pontificate/.

herds with the smell of the sheep and pastoral conversion, Francis has drawn on Aparecida and the CELAM tradition at large. Seeing this clearly helps to understand Francis's take on synodality. It is as far removed from going with the flow as it is from rigidly sticking to church teaching and ecclesial customs; the point is a pastoral conversion that ensures that the church serves the people and facilitates their faith journey. All the rest flows from that: theological reformulations, liturgical inculturation, institutional reform, and so on.[42]

In conclusion, these experiences incline Pope Francis to conversation and consultation, without the usual ecclesial fear of new questions, unexpected perspectives, or different dogmatic convictions. Since his years as a Jesuit superior, pastoral closeness has been the norm, and it has always included the willingness to learn. Since becoming a bishop, he has practiced shared decision-making processes in which it is standard practice to work with a body of consultors. Both intellectually and practically, he is used to dealing with tensions and seemingly unresolved issues. Pope Francis's commitment to the Synod 2021–24 should be seen in this light. Why not practice on the scale of the global church what he has experienced and practiced already at the scale of his diocese and the Latin American continent?

Conclusion

This chapter has provided some historical considerations that explain how synodality emerged. The church can take comfort from the fact that synodality has old roots that can be traced as far back as the Acts of the Apostles. The early church was very much a journeying church. Not unlike the church in our time, it faced new questions, and as different

---

42. See Ivereigh, "Hearing the Spirit in the Assembly of the People," 360–65.

people gave different answers, this came with discord. Importantly, God's Holy Spirit slowly guided the church in the right direction. Moreover, we noted how various ecclesial crises call for synodality. Speaking out with *parrhesia*, humbly listening, and discerning together—all of which characterize synodal ways of proceeding—promote a culture that is radically different from the one in which sexual and financial abuses and scandals continue and careerism and corruption flourish. Finally, we observed how Pope Francis has been a major catalyst in advancing synodality as a valid (and much needed) contemporary ecclesial way of proceeding.

Chapter Three

Snapshots of the Synod on Synodality

The previous chapters explored synodality's theological and historical foundations. We now shift our attention to the recent Synod on Synodality held between 2021 and 2024. This chapter illumines distinctive features of the synod by addressing its goals, style, and manner of proceeding. Six snapshots elucidate important moments in the synod, including the way they shape our appreciation and understanding of synodality writ large. These six moments are: the announcement of the synod logo, the official opening of the synod in Rome, the listening sessions on the local level, the release of the document Enlarge the Space of Your Tent in 2022, the gathering of continental assemblies in early 2023, and the general assembly in Rome in October 2023. These snapshots speak to specific dimensions of synodality, and in doing so, they tie concrete experiences of the synodal process to the style and theological commitments of synodality. As we have discussed in previous chapters, synodality is not, first and foremost, an idea; rather, it is a lived experience and expression of Christian life. Thus, synodality can be appreciated fully only through encountering concrete examples. We therefore approach the Synod on Synodality not merely as a fact of history; rather, we look for the way it illustrates synodality as a lived reality and expresses vital theological priorities.

On October 9, 2021, Pope Francis opened a synod entitled *For a Synodal Church: Communion, Participation, Mission*. This gathering is commonly referred to as the Synod on Synodality. At its heart, this initiative invites the People of God to listen to "what the Spirit is saying to the churches" (Rev 2:7). Many would argue that the initial foundations for this process were laid in an address that came early in Francis's pontificate, one sometimes described as the "magna carta" of synodality. On October 17, 2015, Francis spoke at a ceremony commemorating the fiftieth anniversary of the institution of the Synod of Bishops, the advisory body of bishops established by Paul VI in 1965. Francis's choice of this occasion to announce a priority for his pontificate was intentional. He wanted to link his vision of synodality to the experience of Vatican II and to the regular practice of synods in the church's life. The address introduced and gave meaning to a term that many had never heard of, but which would become a focal point in the church's life in the coming years: synodality. Francis described a synodal church as "a Church which listens, [and] which realizes that listening is more than simply hearing." In such a church there is "a mutual listening in which everyone has something to learn. The faithful people, the college of bishops, the bishop of Rome: all listening to the Holy Spirit, the 'Spirit of truth' (Jn 14:17), in order to know what he says to the Churches (Rev 2:7)." This type of mutual listening is essential because God speaks to us through others and graces us with diverse charisms. In this address, Francis emphasized the importance of journeying together as church, a concept that he noted is simple to articulate but difficult to put into practice. Francis's conclusion was clear: "We must continue along this path. The world in which we live, and which we are called to love and serve, even with its contradictions, demands that the Church strengthen cooperation in all areas of her mission. It is precisely this path of *synodality* which God expects of the Church of the third millennium."[1]

1. Pope Francis, Ceremony Commemorating the 50th Anniversary.

Pope Francis's address signaled that he would be inviting the church to enter an intense period of listening, accompaniment, and renewal. Gathering the church together for this intense process might suggest "introversion" or a time when the church "turns in on itself," but in reality it became one of the greatest consultation efforts in human history.[2] In this process, the church sought to listen to, and involve, the world's 1.36 billion Catholics and, beyond that, the whole world in a collaborative effort to discern the voice of the Holy Spirit and reflect together on its call to the church today. The six snapshots below capture critical elements of how the process unfolded and what they reveal about the nature of a synodal church.

Snapshot #1

The Synod Logo: The Whole Church Underway

---

2. Radcliffe, *Listening Together*, 5.

Our first snapshot is an image: the synod logo. This logo provided important early indications of the Synod on Synodality's style and priorities. The graphic includes fifteen silhouettes of people walking together on a journey. The travelers are diverse, yet they move forward as one. A majestic tree with branches reaching up towards the heavens sets the backdrop for this pilgrimage. The creator of the logo, French artist Isabelle de Senilhes, notes that this "Tree of Life" represents vitality and strength.[3] Its branches extend horizontally, like wings or open hands, suggesting the outreach of the Holy Spirit. The shape of the branches also calls to mind the cross of Jesus and the new life that it brings. This is reminiscent of the tree of life, which in Christian art and literature signifies Christ crucified, from whose cross new, verdant, and creative life flows forth. At its top, the logo's tree carries the Eucharist, which shines down on the travelers like the sun and offers vital food, or "*viaticum*," for the journey. In this image, the tree of life shelters, unites, and sustains the pilgrims beneath it. Under the tree, as its foundations, are the three main themes of the synod: "communion, participation, mission."

This logo conveys powerful realities about the synod without employing complicated theological or technical language. It portrays a differentiated group of people representing the meaning of *synod*: "walking together." The sense of motion in the image underscores synodality as a dynamic rather than static experience. There is no hierarchy among the travelers; they simply accompany each other as people on the way. The bishop pictured in the group moves with the crowd rather than ahead of it, outside of it, or in any way apart from it. The way that the pilgrims walk together signifies that the entire People of God will participate in this synodal journey. Thus, the logo

---

3. The Official Logo of the Synodal Path, https://www.synod.va/en/news/the-official-logo-of-the-synodal-path.html.

marks a significant conceptual shift: the synod will involve all the faithful rather than merely gathering the bishops.

Historically, synods have been meetings where bishops came together to make decisions for the whole church. The synodal tradition from the earliest days of Christianity has emphasized the centrality of episcopal authority, yet it also reflects an abiding belief that each bishop brought his community with him in spirit and, as such, gave instantiation of the whole People of God. In other words, synods or councils have been seen as gatherings of the universal church because the presence of the local shepherds connoted the presence of the people in each local church. The synod logo reframes this ancient sense by providing a visual indication that the People of God will not only be represented symbolically by their bishop but will be physically present, gathered around and in pilgrimage with him.

The synod logo conveys another aspect of the event's uniqueness: its length. At the time of its original release, the graphic included the title "Synod 2021–2023." The fact that the image announced a multi-year event was striking. Since the Second Vatican Council, synods have typically met for short periods of a few weeks or months. These synods typically advised the pope on a particular feature of the church's life or, as we see frequently in the ancient church, met long enough to adjudicate an open theological question. Recent gatherings of the Synod of Bishops have focused on the Eucharist, the family, the Amazonian region, and the situation of youth and young adults. The bishops gathered at those assemblies considered important questions or challenges related to the issue at hand and sought to identify proper pastoral responses. Their primary work often centered on developing, amending, or finalizing a text prepared for the meeting prior to the bishops' arrival. These discrete tasks required a relatively short amount of time. Extending the duration of the upcoming synod from several weeks to two years indicated a shift in the nature of its work. At this gathering, bishops would not be editing a preexisting text, but all the members of the church would try to listen to one another. Therefore, because the nature of the work was different and more people would be involved, more time was needed.

Almost immediately after the synod began in October of 2021, there were calls for adjustments to its timeline. The earliest requests regarded the length of the local phase. The synod's original plan called for the local phase to begin in October 2021 and extend through April 2022. This called for dioceses across the world to hold multiple listening sessions involving the widest possible participation and to harvest what was shared in these sessions in a ten-page report. Several bishops voiced concerns that the time allotted was insufficient to organize the necessary logistics, train facilitators, hold multiple diocesan consultations, and compose a synthesis report. They sought an extension of several months. Other bishops cautioned against such a change, arguing that altering the timeline, especially at such an early stage, would erode people's confidence in the church's ability to plan and execute the overall process. After some consideration, Francis agreed to delay the deadline to August 2022. He noted that synods are about listening and if his brother bishops believed that more time was needed, he would give it to them.

An even more significant shift in the synod's timeline came later, when Francis announced in October 2022 that he was extending the synod for another year and that it would conclude in October 2024 rather than October 2023. Again critiques surfaced that changes in process or timeline could undermine a sense of trust. Yet the decision remained and the dates on the synod logo were updated to read "Synod 2021–2024." While the synod logo is a relatively simple graphic, it provided an early indication of important aspects of this event: broad participation, a shared journey, and flexibility on reaching the destination.

Snapshot #2

The Official Opening of the Synod in Rome:
The Start of Synodal Conversation

The official opening of the synod took place in Rome on October 9 and 10, 2021. This gathering conveys further dimensions of synodality's style and theological commitments. I (Kristin) experienced this as a member of the synod's Theological Commission.

From its outset, Francis and the General Secretariat for the Synod of Bishops rooted the entire process in the practice of *spiritual conversation*, also referred to in official documents as "conversation in the Spirit." Spiritual conversation is not just a discussion of spiritual topics; it is a method of group dialogue involving several rounds of active listening, intentional speaking, pausing for silence, and discerning the voice of the Holy Spirit among the group. For the bishops, theologians, and lay people present at the solemn opening, even the selection of meeting spaces demonstrated the nature of spiritual conversation and the overall shape of synodality. Typically, synods convened after Vatican II have conducted much of their work in the Synod Aula, a large auditorium with a speakers' table at the front and seating graded away from it in degrees. In architectural terms, this is largely a passive space designed so that select individuals at the front can speak while the rest of the participants receive information. However, in the fall of 2021, time spent in the aula was limited, and instead we gathered in small breakout rooms fitted with tables arranged in a circle. This venue change concretely reflected the dynamic sharing sought by synodal listening, as opposed to a process rooted in passive reception and the production of documents. In short, *where* we met conveyed a great deal about *what* we were there to do.

Spiritual conversation seeks to heighten awareness of and sensitivity to the Holy Spirit. Christina Kheng of Singapore, a leader on the synod's Methodology Commission, notes that spiritual conversation rests "upon a theological worldview which acknowledges God's Spirit present in all of creation." It receives further foundation and authority from the church's belief in the dignity and co-responsibility of the baptized. These commitments ground a view that "everyone's voice deserves an equal chance to be heard and to be assured of a welcoming, engaged, and respectful reception." Not premised on purely rational arguments or oriented towards conveying linear information, spiritual conversation, Kheng writes, "engages the whole human person including their intellectual, social, affective, and spiritual dimensions."[4] This method of exchange invites participants to let go of their attachments and preference for a particular outcome and open themselves to the prompting of the Spirit. The aim of this process is that, when the group reaches its decision, the participants can share the fruits of discernment echoing the words from the Acts of the Apostles: "It seemed good to the Holy Spirit and to us . . ." (Acts 15:28).

Kheng provides a helpful summary of the various steps of spiritual conversation and a brief orientation for each element. She names seven steps of this method:

1. **Individual preparation:** Participants are provided with relevant information and questions for discernment. Each person prepares by reading, reflecting, and praying with the material, in order to get in touch with his or her personal experiences, viewpoints, and feelings, and thereby to discern what the Holy Spirit might be revealing.

---

4. Christina Kheng, "The Method is the Message: Method of Spiritual Conversation," in *The People of God Have Spoken: Continental Ecclesial Assemblies with the Synod on Synodality*, ed. Myriam Wijlens and Vimal Tirimanna, CSsR (Dublin: Columba Books, 2023), 28.

2. **Gathering:** Participants then gather in small groups at a conducive place and set aside appropriate time to carry out three rounds of sharing.

3. **Round One:** Every person receives equal time (usually two to five minutes) to share the fruits of their prayer and reflection. As each shares, the others listen deeply without interrupting; they attend not only to what is said but also to the feelings and inner movements within the speaker as well as themselves and the group. Everyone gives the speaker full and undivided attention, setting aside preoccupations about what to say or how to respond. Listeners also refrain from giving advice, making comments, answering questions, or raising new inquiries. They should listen for God.

4. **Silent pause:** A silent pause of two to three minutes follows the first round so that participants can probe what they heard in the first round, how it affected them, and what other significant movements they sensed. These might include deep joy, energy, enthusiasm, hope, gratitude, and inner peace, or anger, despondency, hopelessness, languor, and even tension or confusion.

5. **Round Two:** Participants share the fruits of their silent reflection on the points raised during the first round. Everyone listens to each speaker attentively. This is not a time to share additional information that one would have liked to have included in the first round. It focuses on reflecting more deeply on the movements that were sparked by that round. The movement seeks depth in reflection rather than breadth in additional information.

6. **Silent pause:** Another time of silence follows. Participants seek to discern what the Holy Spirit seems to be revealing to the group through what has been shared.

This often resonates with what stirs them most deeply, what brings new insight or interior conversion, what invokes authentic commitment, what themes seem to recur frequently, what beckons further attention however subtly, or even new questions that arise.

7. **Round Three:** Every participant shares the fruits of their silent reflection. The group seeks to identify key points and interior movements that have arisen. It is not enough to list the points mentioned most often. Rather, discernment is needed, which also pays attention to marginal and prophetic voices.[5]

The structured nature of spiritual conversation promotes an equality of exchange and creates space for authentic listening. It does not seek technical proficiency. Rather, it shapes people's attitudes and attentiveness to each other and to the Holy Spirit.

At the formal opening of the synod in Rome, all participants—bishops, members of the four commissions (theology, methodology, spirituality, and communication), lay leaders, young adults, and facilitators from across the globe—gathered together to engage in spiritual conversation. After beginning in the aula, the groups proceeded to breakout rooms organized by language. I participated in one of the English-language groups. It included cardinals from several different countries; young women from New Zealand, India, and Mexico; a journalist from Africa; leaders of worldwide lay movements; and a facilitator. The facilitator asked us to reflect on and respond

5. Kheng, "Method is the Message," 25–26. Kheng's list has been slightly modified here. The practice of spiritual conversation is also presented in section A.2 of the *Instrumentum Laboris* 2023 for the XVI Ordinary General Assembly. See page 78 of this book for a graphic illustration of this practice.

to this question: "What is the Holy Spirit calling the church to today?" Each person was given two minutes to share. At the two-minute mark, the facilitator gently brought the person's contribution to a close no matter who was speaking.

At the end of our time together, we all affirmed the sacred and transformative nature of the method of spiritual conversation. Through this process, we glimpsed what it means to move from *I* to *we*. Our experience provided evidence of Pope Francis's statement in *Evangelii Gaudium*: "When we live out a spirituality of drawing nearer to others and seeking their welfare, our hearts are opened wide to the Lord's greatest and most beautiful gifts. Whenever we encounter another person in love, we learn something new about God. Whenever our eyes are opened to acknowledge the other, we grow in the light of faith and knowledge of God."[6] We learned, as one theologian observed, that "to listen is to emulate God's own fundamental disposition towards people."[7]

The synod's opening session thus provides a snapshot of the way that synodality, through the practice of spiritual conversation, allows the People of God to better attune themselves to the voice of the Holy Spirit working in the church today. Its approach would mark the way later synodal sessions would be conducted, including the sessions in Rome in October 2023 and 2024, as we will comment in Snapshot 6.

6. Pope Francis, Apostolic Exhortation *Evangelii Gaudium* 272, November 24, 2014, https://www.vatican.va/content/francesco/en/apost_exhortations /documents/papa-francesco_esortazione-ap_20131124_evangelii-gaudium .html. Hereafter, EG.

7. Susan Bigelow Reynolds, "Are We Protagonists Yet? The Place of Women in the Synod's Working Document," *Commonweal*, December 9, 2022, https://www.commonwealmagazine.org/women-church-synod-francis -catholic.

04

The conversation in the Spirit
A dynamic of discernment in the synodal Church

PERSONAL PREPARATION

By entrusting oneself to the Father, conversing in prayer with the Lord Jesus and listening to the Holy Spirit, each one prepares his or her own contribution to the question about which he or she is called to discern.

Silence, prayer and listening to the Word of God

« Taking the word and listening »

Each person takes turns speaking from his or her own experience and prayer, and listens carefully to the contribution of others.

Silence and Prayer

« Making space for others & the Other»

From what the others have said, each one shares what has resonated most with him or her or what has aroused the most resistance in him or her, allowing himself or herself to be guided by the Holy Spirit: "When, listening, did my heart burn in my chest?"

Silence and Prayer

« Building together »

Together we dialogue on the basis of what emerged earlier in order to discern and gather the fruit of the conversation in the Spirit: to recognize intuitions and convergences; to identify discordances, obstacles and new questions; to allow prophetic voices to emerge. It is important that everyone can feel represented by the outcome of the work. " To what steps is the Holy Spirit calling us together?"

FINAL PRAYER OF THANKSGIVING

for further information
www.synod.va

Snapshot #3

Listening at the Local Level:
Diocesan and National Syntheses

The first phase of the synod unfolded at the diocesan or local level between October 2021 and August 2022. Pope Francis and the General Secretariat for the Synod called every diocese in the world to hold listening sessions, with the goal of obtaining the widest possible participation. Organizers were instructed to reach out beyond regular Mass-goers and invite those who had left the church, who felt excluded, and whose voices are not often heard. The *Vademecum* states, "While all the baptized are specifically called to take part in the Synodal Process, no one—no matter their religious affiliation—should be excluded from sharing their perspective and experiences, insofar as they want to help the Church on her synodal journey of seeking what is good and true. This is especially true of those who are most vulnerable or marginalized." The *Vademecum* also encouraged that "special care should be taken to involve those persons who may risk being excluded: women, the handicapped, refugees, migrants, the elderly, people who live in poverty, Catholics who rarely or never practice their faith, etc. Creative means should also be found in order to involve children and youth."[8] In these listening sessions, no topics were out of bounds. Rather, the faithful were invited to speak freely and with *parrhesia*.

The synodal method sees listening at the local level as a necessary initial step on the journey. The local church constitutes the concrete locus in which the faithful gather to hear the Scriptures proclaimed, celebrate the Eucharist, and live out their lives of faith and discipleship. Some dioceses throughout the world expended tremendous efforts to create listening sessions, rooted in the method of spiritual conversation, that

8. General Secretariat for the Synod, *Vademecum* 2.1.

would allow for authentic exchanges. Communities made significant investments in discerning how to create an atmosphere of trust, prayer, and authentic exchange so that all, perhaps especially those who felt excluded or judged by the church, would feel comfortable sharing their experiences. Leaders realized that an invitation to "come back" or "come talk" would be insufficient in itself to persuade those bearing wounds to return. Listening sessions around the world took a variety of forms, including large group sessions, small group sessions, one-on-one conversations, and virtual opportunities to offer thoughts. This monumental process created many of its forms and practices from scratch while executing them in a tight timeframe; this led many to liken this phase of the synod to "trying to build a plane while flying it."

The experience of the synod varied greatly across local and national churches; some had a robust, transformative process while others barely registered the synod's existence. Throughout the local/national phase, I (Kristin) traveled around the United States as an ambassador for the synod and encountered people excited and energized by this process as well as critics, skeptics, and people eager for more information. From my time on college campuses, in parishes, and working with numerous Catholic organizations, journalists, and religious communities, I developed a list of the five most common questions that I was asked at this stage of the synodal journey:

- "What can I do if my priest or bishop is not doing anything about the synod?"

- "Why should I participate in the synod? How do I know that my voice will matter?"

- "I was really excited when Pope Francis said that the synod process would seek out those who have left the church, those excluded from the church, those whose voices are often not heard by the church. Why don't I see more of those efforts?"

- "How can we be a synodal church if women are excluded from leadership roles and from nearly all processes of decision-making?"

- "How do we know that when it comes to writing the final report, the bishops won't filter out the most important things that are communicated in the listening sessions, especially calls for greater inclusion?"

These same questions arose across diverse cities and demographics. They testify to a shared experience of a church that does not always listen and/or respond meaningfully. These questions are also striking in their honesty. They give voice to real and deeply felt concerns. Importantly, they also reflect hope in the Spirit's abiding presence and that the synodal journey, properly embraced, might bring authentic renewal to the church.

The synod tasked every diocese with synthesizing the fruit of the completed listening sessions into a ten-page report. Composing these reports presented a huge challenge for dioceses, many of which had generated thousands of pages of documents capturing listening session content. The task of distilling the listening sessions into a cogent and authentic summary felt overwhelming for many local leaders. When complete, the local diocese or ecclesial body submitted their report to the appropriate episcopal body.

Next, the episcopal bodies took the ten-page diocesan submissions they received and synthesized them into a ten-page national report. The magnitude of this work was not the same in every country. For example, the United States had to summarize over two hundred diocesan reports, while Liberia had only three to include, even as they had the same ten-page limit. In producing summaries of the listening sessions, leaders at both the diocesan and national levels had to avoid creating a "summary of summaries" that lost the vibrancy and authenticity of people's voices in the weeds of data collection or empirical analysis. Instead, the national reports that culminated the local phase needed to reflect the overall aim of the synod: careful listening to what the Holy Spirit was saying to the churches.

Snapshot #4

Enlarge the Space of Your Tent:
Hearing the Voices of the People of God

At the conclusion of the local phase, Rome received 112 national reports, as well as additional reports from the Eastern Catholic Churches (15) and various dicasteries of the Roman Curia (18). The Secretariat of the Synod appointed a group comprised of three people from each continent to synthesize these texts into one document. I (Kristin) served as one of the representatives appointed from North America. What resulted from this group's work was the Document for the Continental Stage, also known by its title, Enlarge the Space of Your Tent.[9] (The title is taken from Isaiah 54:2 and evokes the biblical sense of a tent as "a space of *communion*, a place of *participation*, and a foundation for *mission*."[10]) This document provides wonderful insight into the nature of synodality. It is different from any other text issued by the Vatican, because it draws on the voices of the People of God as its sole authority.

Enlarge the Space of Your Tent distills a number of major themes from the global listening sessions and offers them back to the People of God for further discernment. The style is dialogical. It does not offer data or analysis; it says to the local churches around the world: "This is what we heard you say." It also asks the faithful: "Where have we heard you correctly,

---

9. It can be found at https://www.synod.va/content/dam/synod/common/phases/continental-stage/dcs/Documento-Tappa-Continentale-EN.pdf.

10. Document for the Continental Stage 11.

and where have we missed things, underestimated concerns, or overstated realities?" Later in chapter four we will identify several key themes that surfaced throughout this consultation; the focus here will be on the unique style of this text and the way that it lifts up the voices of the People of God.

The work of writing Enlarge the Space of Your Tent was completed in a retreat-like atmosphere in Frascati, Italy, about forty miles outside of Rome. The gathering was intentionally held away from the Eternal City so that the writers would immerse themselves in the process without temptation to duck out to attend "just one" meeting or teach "just one" class. At our first session, Cardinal Mario Grech, General Secretary of the Synod of Bishops, laid out the task. He told us that we were gathered to be "the heart and ears of the church, to hear the cry of the People of God."[11] Grech said that the national reports were a form of sacred sharing and that it would be a significant failure if we did not honor the work, time, openness, and trust that had gone into the process that produced them. Grech added that we would fail if we did not listen to the voices of the People of God but only heard what we wanted or expected to hear, or if we rushed to explain what the People of God meant or why they spoke as they did. Such a failure, he said, would in fact be a "sin," because it would squander a unique opportunity to hear what God is revealing to the churches.

We sought to open ourselves to this work in a variety of ways. Foremost among these was following the method of spiritual conversation for all our discussions and punctuating our daily activities with prayer. There was no writing for the

---

11. Author's notes from meeting in Frascati, Italy, on September 21, 2022. See also Austen Ivereigh, "I Helped Write the First Global Synod Document: Here's What We Heard from Catholics around the World," *America*, October 27, 2022, https://www.americamagazine.org/faith/2022/10/27/frascati-document-synod-synodality-244031.

first several days, only listening to one another, rereading the texts, and prayer. When we turned to drafting the document, we were careful to keep the actual words of the reports at the forefront. Every time someone suggested a point for inclusion in the text, the first question was, "Where are the quotes that support it?" A constant refrain among the writers was, "Show me the quotes." We strove to root the text in ideas expressed by the People of God and to balance our use of language and quotations from diverse corners of the world church. We also prioritized an awareness of the voices absent from the document. We kept an empty chair in the room to keep our minds attuned to those individuals and groups whose perspectives might not be featured in our text, either because they had not contributed to the original reports or because, for one reason or another, their voices did not command the same kind of attention. Some of those we could imagine in the empty chair were priests, bishops, young people, the elderly, and Catholics who have concerns about the reforms of Vatican II. In Frascati, recognizing silence was another form of listening.

Enlarge the Space of Your Tent expresses the joys and hopes, the griefs and anguish of the People of God in their own words. Voices from every part of the globe share their sense of where the Holy Spirit is calling the church today. These voices express deep love for the church as well as clear and firm convictions about what needs to change.

To honor these voices, Enlarge the Space of Your Tent adopts a unique style. On the one hand, it avoids merely repeating what the reports said. On the other hand, it avoids a rush to problem-solving. Instead, it seeks to lift up the voices of the People of God and offer back to them their own words as a tool for discernment. The text contains no quotes from Pope Francis (or any pope), Vatican II, or any magisterial document, stressing a distinct methodological approach. It undertakes no technical descriptions of theological concepts such as the *sensus fidelium*, baptismal ecclesiology, or episcopal collegiality. Ultimately, Enlarge the Space of Your Tent demonstrates the church's capacity to listen. It accepts the entire People of God as witnesses by listening globally, embracing a dialogical style, and demonstrating genuine openness to the movement of the Spirit.[12] Synodal texts teach best by expressing lived realities. Rather than prescribing what the church *should* do, this document tries to *do* it. Rather than simply exhorting us to listen to global voices, it actively listens to (and reflects) these voices.

Enlarge the Space of Your Tent constitutes a significant milestone in ecclesial listening. By sharing the authentic testimony of the People of God, the church shows a readiness to listen and a commitment to attend to what it heard. Susan Bigelow Reynolds of Emory University notes, "What is included in [Enlarge the Space of Your Tent] is stunning not because it conveys new truths but because these well-known truths are being voiced in such a document." She adds, "There is an accountability to history that comes from committing these reports to print."[13]

Sarah Larson, executive director of Awake Milwaukee, a lay-led advocacy group that supports survivors of clergy sexual abuse, noted that Enlarge the Space of Your Tent certainly "reflects the experience of Awake and the contribution we submitted from our own synodal conversations with abuse survivors and others who care about this issue."[14] Larson's comment confirms the authenticity of the text and the way

12. Carolyn Weir Herman, "What the Synod Doc Says about Women, and What It Could Mean for the Future of the Church," *America*, May 12, 2023, https://www.americamagazine.org/faith/2023/05/12/synodality -women-church-herman-245208.

13. Reynolds, "Are We Protagonists Yet?"

14. Brian Fraga, "Vatican's New Synod Document Draws Praise for Its Signs of Listening," *National Catholic Reporter*, October 27, 2022, https:// www.ncronline.org/news/vaticans-new-synod-document-draws-praise-its -signs-listening.

that people, even those who had long felt ignored by the church, sensed that the church was truly listening.

A final affirmation of the uniqueness of Enlarge the Space of Your Tent comes from Carolyn Weir Herman, who notes that it "indicates a new way of proceeding for the Catholic Church, one that comes from genuine listening, honest dialogue and discerning consultation of all the people of God." She goes on to state that the document "gives witness to the *sensus fidelium*, which emerges from ecclesial consultation of all the baptized, not only from the episcopal consultation of the ordained. It cites quotations that allow 'the voices of the People of God from all parts of the world [to] speak as much as possible on their own terms and find resonance.'"[15]

Enlarge the Space of Your Tent is the document of a listening church. If we can "know a tree by its fruit" (see Matt 7:16-20), then we can look at this document and say that it is the product of a church that is ready to listen and prioritizes accompaniment.

Snapshot #5

Trying Out New Ecclesial Structures:
The Continental Assemblies

In a process filled with innovations, firsts, and surprises, one of the most significant developments of the Synod on Synodality involved the introduction of a continental-level phase of discernment. The introduction of this phase engages one of synodality's central aims: discerning how the church can coordinate listening and decision-making between the various levels of its life—local, regional, and universal. This type of consultation enhances the symphonic listening and accountability demanded by synodality. Chapter seven will

---

15. Herman, "What the Synod Doc Says about Women."

explore the structural implications of creating regional-level discernment. What follows here is a snapshot of how this type of listening unfolded during the Synod on Synodality.

As we saw above, Enlarge the Space of Your Tent synthesized the contributions made by the People of God on the local level. The process of determining the fruits of the synod's local phase could have ended there. Yet the Secretariat for the Synod, with Francis's approval, recognized the need for a *restitutio*: "a giving back to the people what had been collected, summarized and synthesized."[16] Accordingly, the Secretariat decided to send Enlarge the Space of Your Tent back to the churches, this time gathered as continents, for another stage of listening and discernment. Through this process, continental assemblies would help determine the extent to which Enlarge the Space of Your Tent resonated with the voices of the People of God and what revisions, additions, or omissions might be necessary. Myriam Wijlens, a Dutch theologian and consultor for the synod, and Vimal Tirimanna, a Redemptorist priest from Sri Lanka who is also a voting delegate for the synod, noted that the secretariat was also motivated by a sense that "the People of God locally should listen to what the People of God in other parts of the world had heard while listening to the Holy Spirit. A kind of becoming aware of the others and mutual reception between the different local churches in different continents should be provided for."[17]

The Catholic communities of some continents, notably Latin America, had extensive experience discerning together, while others, notably North America and Europe, did not. The Vatican did not dictate how these consultations should unfold.

---

16. Miriam Wijlens and Vimal Tirimanna CSsR, "Introduction," in *People of God Have Spoken*, 11. On this topic see also Rafael Luciani, "La *restitutio* al pueblo de Dios latinoamericano y caribeño: 'Lo que afecta a todos debe ser tratado y aprobado por todos,'" *Revista CLAR* 61/2 (2023): 14–29.

17. Wijlens and Tirimanna, "Introduction," 11.

Instead, it allowed church leadership of various continents a great deal of flexibility in designing their assemblies, offering only two guidelines: first, the gatherings had to employ the method of spiritual conversation, and second, they had to include diverse sectors of the People of God so that the meetings would reflect local practices, cultural and language elements, geography, and logistics within each continent. The fact that the Vatican allowed this level of freedom and difference in the methods used by various regions is itself a notable and unique aspect of this synodal process.

Each of the seven continents organized its assembly differently, and, as such, they produced seven examples of how continent-level discernment can occur.[18] For example, North America, with only two episcopal conferences—the United States Conference of Catholic Bishops (USCCB) and the Canadian Catholic Conference of Bishops (CCCB)—was the only continent to conduct its gathering virtually.[19] This method allowed a large number of delegates (931) to participate but did not offer the experiences of an in-person gathering with shared meals, worship, and spontaneous conversations. On the other hand, the European assembly, comprised of 39 episcopal conferences, met in a hybrid mode in Prague with 182 delegates in-person and an additional 269 online. In addition to navigating the complexities of integrating the contributions of in-person and online participants, this gathering had to manage working in five languages, finding words and phrasing that could convey the same meaning across all of them. The

18. For an excellent account of the methods and findings of the continental assemblies, see Wijlens and Tirimanna, *People of God Have Spoken.* Each chapter is dedicated to exploring how one of the continental assemblies unfolded.

19. While Mexico is geographically a part of North America, the church of Mexico participated in the synod's continental phase as part of the Latin American and Caribbean region, given Mexico's long history of partnership and ongoing work on several Encuentros with the Latin American and Caribbean Episcopal Council better known as CELAM.

Asian continental assembly met in-person in Bangkok. Eighty delegates included the bishop of each diocese accompanied by two other representatives.

The wisdom gleaned from the successes and challenges of these seven continental ecclesial assemblies stands, in itself, as a remarkable fruit of the synod process. Archbishop Timothy Costello of Perth, Australia, a participant in the Oceania meetings and one of the synod's official consultors, observed that the differences in the style of these assemblies underscores the reality that "there is more than one way of being the Church."[20] Each continent synthesized its findings in a report submitted to the Vatican; these seven reports would become the basis for the working document, or *Instrumentum Laboris*, that served as the basis of the Ordinary Assembly in Rome in October 2023, the synod's universal phase.[21]

The synod is about listening and finding new ways to listen. At the heart of the synod lay questions about how the church journeys together on different levels—local, regional/continental, and universal—and how these different levels provide distinctive opportunities for the church to advance the mission entrusted to it. The experience of the continental ecclesial assemblies in the spring of 2023 speaks to these questions. The synod's continental phase brought to life structures that had never existed before but which have the capacity to serve the church in meaningful ways. This snapshot provides a powerful example of the church's eagerness to try out new structures for listening and of the creativity that is inherent to synodality.

20. Bernadette M. Reis, FSP, "Synod Continental Stage: 'Most Innovative Aspect of Synodal Process,'" *Vatican News*, April 20, 2023, https://www.vaticannews.va/en/vatican-city/news/2023-04/synod-continental-stage-conclusion-press-conference.html.

21. The *Instrumentum Laboris* for the first general assembly of the Synod on Synodality can be found at https://www.synod.va/en/news/the-vademecum-for-the-synod-on-synodality.html.

Snapshot #6

*The General Assembly in Rome:
Participatory Decision-Making*

A final snapshot comes from the Ordinary General Assemblies of the Synod (2023 and 2024) and the way that their proceedings adopted new modes of participation and decision-making. Three features of these gatherings come to the fore: 1) the expansion of voting to include women; 2) the inclusion of worksheets to guide the deliberations; and 3) the use of round tables. We begin with the extension of voting in the assemblies.

In April of 2023, the Secretariat of the Synod made the unprecedented announcement that the synod would expand membership in its general assemblies, and thus voting rights, to seventy non-bishops. The Secretariat of the Synod asked each continent to consult its episcopal conferences and develop a list of twenty potential delegates. The request specified that special care should be given to including the names of young people and that at least fifty percent of the individuals put forward should be women. Pope Francis then chose ten delegates from each continent's list of twenty. This decision ensured that a significant number of women would vote at a synod for the first time in history. Prior to this announcement, the "stained-glass ceiling" had received a small but significant crack with the appointment of Nathalie Becquart, a French sister who is a member of the Congregation of Xavières, as the undersecretary of the General Secretariat of the Synod. According to its official constitution, undersecretaries are considered members of the synod assembly and thus have a right to vote. Ultimately, with Pope Francis's initiative, fifty-three women joined Becquart in voting as part of the assembly.

The expansion of voting at the October 2023 assemblies is both a fruit and a seed, a reflection of how things have already changed in the church and a catalyst for future change. The decision to include more diverse participation in ecclesial decision-making was not an entirely new initiative introduced by Rome; instead, it was, in many ways, a reflection of the fact that attitudes and practices in the church had already shifted. Reflecting on how synods function, Christine Schenk wrote, "Change doesn't happen because of a two-thirds favorable vote. A two-thirds vote only ratifies a change that has already occurred."[22]

This is not to dismiss the magnitude of the decision to expand voting rights at the synod. Allowing non-bishops, and especially women, to vote constitutes a seed that will grow and give generations of Catholics the opportunity to see people like themselves participating in the church's life at the highest levels. Importantly, changing who can vote at the synod is not purely an administrative matter; it reflects core principles of synodality. It would be inconsistent, and somewhat incoherent, to have the synodal process unfold as it did—both in terms of its practical dimensions and theological commitments—and then have the voting at the general assembly in Rome restricted to bishops. The goals of the synod would largely ring hollow if the process reached the moment of voting and the synodal transformation of the church did not extend that far. We expect that this decision will not easily be reversed. It will be hard to say at the next synod, "This time around, we don't need women to participate" or "Women's perspectives aren't valuable on this topic." Most importantly, the church will not want to make such a reversal in the future because after benefitting from a greater diversity of participation, it will not want to impoverish itself by its absence.

---

22. Christine Schenk, "When a Female Lens Is Added to the Equation, Something New Can Happen," *National Catholic Reporter*, May 9, 2023, https://www.ncronline.org/opinion/ncr-voices/when-female-lens-added -equation-something-new-can-happen.

A second move towards greater participation in the Synod's General Assembly is seen in the style of the working document prepared for it, the *Instrumentum Laboris*. This text unfolds in two halves. The first half reflects on the experience of being a synodal church, the priorities articulated by the People of God, and what the process yielded in terms of ecclesial self-understanding. The second half introduces a major breakthrough in style and deserves our attention. It articulates the priorities identified by the People of God not as stances or assertions but as *questions*. These questions were posed to the synodal assembly so that it might engage "the task of discerning the concrete steps which enable the continued growth of the synodal church."[23] Groundbreaking and genre-defining is the fact that the *Instrumentum Laboris* explores the priorities advanced by the People of God through a series of fifteen *worksheets*. Its questions illustrate the nature of a listening church, even at a seminal event such as a major synod gathering. The following questions from the worksheets exemplify its style:

- "How can we create spaces where those who feel hurt by the Church and unwelcomed by the community feel recognized, received, free to ask questions and not judged?"

- "How can the Church remain in dialogue with the world without becoming worldly?"

- "Most of the Continental Assemblies and the syntheses of several Episcopal Conferences call for the question of women's inclusion in the diaconate to be considered. Is it possible to envisage this, and in what way?"

---

23. *Instrumentum Laboris* 2023, 10.

- "Should Bishops discern together with or separately from the other members of the People of God? Do both options (together and separately) have a place in a synodal Church?"

- "When might a Bishop feel obliged to take a decision that differs from the considered advice offered by the consultative bodies? What would be the basis for such a decision?"[24]

Often in the past, the church avoided raising questions that it could not answer, seemingly out of a fear that asking a question without immediately providing an answer made the church look weak or uncertain. Recall that past synods gathered in order for bishops to edit or provide further shape to a text prepared in advance of the assembly. Such a procedure allows for contributions but significantly limits what the body can decide and accomplish. The fact that the work of the 2023 general assembly used the format of worksheets underscores that the assembly itself would be the productive body.

The use of worksheets and expressing what the listening church heard in the form of questions rather than definitive statements conveys something powerful about the work of the extraordinary assembly and the nature of authority in a synodal church. Worksheets do not say, "I have all the answers." Instead, they typically present questions; they invite reflection and responses. To this end, the *Instrumentum Laboris* 2023 states that the worksheets are "to be done" and not "to be read."[25] This affirms the synod as an active and participatory process. It is not about affirming predetermined agendas or engaging in token consultations. On this shift, Michael Sean

---

24. These questions are taken from the *Instrumentum Laboris* 2023, pp. 30, 36, 42, 46, and 46.

25. *Instrumentum Laboris* 2023, p. 24.

Winters wrote, "Predetermined results? For the first time, the *Instrumentum Laboris* does not present a draft of a final document for the synodal assembly to amend, but a series of questions. These questions reflect those raised in the worldwide consultations. The planning committee did not draft a set of plausible responses. It did not lean into the neuralgic issues one way or the other. It acknowledges them and, in doing so, also acknowledges that the effort to declare some topics closed failed to stop the questioning."[26] The *Instrumentum Laboris* 2023 introduced a new style of being church; its attempts to guide the assembly by questions and worksheets reflect an effort to take baptismal dignity seriously.

A third feature of this gathering that supported new modes of participation and decision-making was the use of round tables. As was mentioned in the second snapshot above, in the years after Vatican II, synods typically met in an auditorium-style room with the participants seated in rows of chairs facing a dais. The synod's general assembly in October of 2023 introduced a decisive innovation. The participants at this event gathered around round tables. Each of these tables had seats for eleven people who, notably, did not sit according to rank or in any type of hierarchical order. This synod drew its inspiration from events such as the Australian plenary council and the Asian continental assembly, both of which had used this type of seating to support the practice of spiritual conversation and reflect the dignity of all before God. Cardinal Jean-Claude Hollerich, the relator-general of the synod, called this development part of the "new grammar of synodality." He noted that "just like the grammar of our languages changes as they develop, so does the grammar of synodality: It changes with time." Hollerich also added that the use of round tables re-

---

26. Michael Sean Winters, "Synodal Working Document Is Deeply Rooted in Vatican II," *National Catholic Reporter*, June 26, 2023, https://www.ncronline.org/opinion/ncr-voices/synodal-working-document-deeply-rooted-vatican-ii.

minds us "that none of us is a star at the synod" and the only true protagonist is the Holy Spirit.[27]

The "new grammar" of the round tables helped to facilitate the mutual listening and sharing of experiences sought by the synod. The image of the synod participants, including the pope, sitting around round tables provides one of the most powerful representations of the true nature of the synod. In fact, John Allen Jr., a leading Catholic journalist from the United States, stated that the synod on synodality might come to be known as the "table synod" and that the most powerful

27. Quoted in Jonathan Liedel, "New 'Grammar of Synodality' on Display at the Start of Synod Gathering," Catholic News Agency, October 4, 2023, https://www.catholicnewsagency.com/news/255577/new-grammar -of-synodality-on-display-at-start-of-synod-gathering.

legacy of this gathering might be its innovative style of meeting.[28] The use of round tables was a concrete effort to decentralize decision-making and engage in authentic discernment where all voices are heard. As we see in the images below, *where* the synod participants meet says a lot about our view of the church, the way that we understand authority, and how we view co-responsibility.

Conclusion

These snapshots of the Synod on Synodality 2021–24 offer glimpses of the event itself, and they also reveal a great deal about the style and goals of synodality. No group of snapshots could exhaust the reality of this event, yet taken as a mosaic, they illumine important aspects of how a synodal church walks together. They show us that synodality is a consultative process that seeks to involve the entire People of God. They also demonstrate that synodality is a creative process that introduces new realities into the church both in terms of structures and in terms of practices and habits. Synodality seeks ways that individuals and communities can attune themselves to the Holy Spirit and thereby become responsive to new promptings of the Spirit. Synodality often surprises us by breaking from previous patterns and creating something new. This means that we cannot determine our path forward as a synodal church by only or primarily constructing blueprints inspired by theoretical ideas. Rather, as these snapshots confirm, a synodal church listens, discerns, creates anew, and revises as part of walking together into the future.

---

28. John Allen Jr., "Just How Valuable Is Sitting at Round Tables?," *Catholic Herald*, October 28, 2023, https://catholicherald.co.uk/just-how-valuable-is-sitting-around-tables/.

Chapter Four

What the Listening Church Heard

Emerging Topics

After exploring some of the major moments and foundations of the synodal process, we shift to considering what the People of God said during this massive consultation. How did the faithful respond when invited to share their sense of where the Holy Spirit is calling the church? What topics emerged? Of course, a comprehensive account of all that was shared during this massive, global consultation is impossible. But it is possible to identify consistent themes and the presence of prophetic voices within the local, national, and continental phases of the process. Here we will consider five key topics that emerged from the reports: the need for formation, a desire for a more welcoming church, synodality as central to the church's nature, the centrality of the liturgy, and the role of women.

Before examining these topics, it is important to highlight two characteristics of the contributions from this multi-year worldwide consultation. These characteristics shape the overall response of the People of God and provide lenses for approaching particular points of content.

First, *the church heard new things*. This was only possible thanks to the synod's unique style, which significantly expanded participation and cultivated equality among speakers. Between 2021 and 2024, the church listened widely and invited people to speak with *parrhesia*. As the comment of Sara Larson in the previous chapter illustrates, many groups and individuals who had long lamented the church's failure to listen to their experiences felt motivated to participate and empowered to share in courageous ways. The global scale of the church's listening made it possible to hear resonances and patterns that had previously gone undetected. By expanding the boundaries of who could speak and keeping all topics on the table, the church created a space where it could hear things that it had never heard before.

Second, these contributions were marked by *a widespread consensus on a variety of topics*. The national reports from across the globe reflect an astounding agreement about the church's joys and challenges. Speaking from my own experience, when I (Kristin) began to read the national reports in preparation for helping to write the global synthesis document, Enlarge the Space of Your Tent, I approached them with trepidation. I expected radical differences among what people in various parts of the world identified as the church's greatest needs and most important priorities. I was nervous about how the writing team would determine which concerns to include in the synthesis and danger of choosing "winners and losers" among them. My anticipation of these problems was fueled, in part, by a long-standing a perception in North America and Europe that the church cannot move too quickly on certain issues, particularly those related to morality, that are often considered vital by believers there, because Catholics in other parts of the world do not view them with the same sense of need or urgency. My worries quickly evaporated when I began reading the reports. What I found was that report after report featured voices from across continents echoing similar dreams and laments for the church.

Anna Rowlands, a key advisor to the synod, shared a similar experience. She noted, "In the early months of the synod, several journalists said that the synod process would inevitably reveal a church divided culturally between Europe and Africa, between clergy and laity, and at war with itself over moral issues." These same journalists, Rowlands observed, had also warned that "the reports had probably all been pre-written, and that the process would be either a sell-out or a stitch-up." After spending time with these texts, Rowlands said that she could confidently tell these journalists that "their preconceptions were wrong." She noted that the reports clarified that "[t]he questions of the status and participation of women, increased transparency in the church, and how to hold together love, mercy and truth in extending a welcome were not solely the concerns of the global North. These echoed from every corner of the Catholic world."[1] She observed that the divisions that surfaced in the reports did not reveal an intercontinental culture war; instead, they typically reflected long-standing disputes within communities that have been shaped by their particular histories. Ultimately, the national syntheses did not paint a picture of a church that is culturally, dogmatically, or theologically divided between the northern and southern hemispheres; they revealed a universal church that shares many of the same wounds and hopes.

Austen Ivereigh, a UK-based Roman Catholic journalist and author who contributed to Enlarge the Space of Your Tent, argues that the consensus found in the global reports should be seen as a manifestation of the *sensus fidei*. On his experience of reading these reports, he wrote,

1. Anna Rowlands, "The Synod Has Taught Me: Catholics Are Not as Divided as the Skeptics Thought," *America*, June 29, 2023, https://www.americamagazine.org/faith/2023/06/29/synod-synodality-polarization-lessons-245554.

In what emerged, I began to grasp the truth of what Pope
Francis says in "Evangelii Gaudium," that "God furnishes
the totality of the faithful with an instinct of faith—*sensus
fidei*—which helps them to discern what is truly of God."
It is an instinct that comes, the pope goes on, with a certain kind of wisdom, "to grasp those realities intuitively,
even when they lack the wherewithal to give them precise
expression." What the Spirit was saying to the church was,
after all, right there in the reports, in that "instinct of
faith" in the voices pained by fragmentation and division,
that longed for a maternal, embracing, patient, more capa-
cious church, one that could gather in those left outside,
one that was better capable of holding in tension difference and disagreement and that takes seriously the idea
that all the baptized are called to mission and to sit at the
table where decisions are discerned.[2]

Ivereigh suggests that the reports portray the People of God
as "on the move" in response to the prompting of the Holy
Spirit. The synodal task, then, is to "help the church to move
with it."[3]

Helping the church to move with the Spirit requires an
understanding of the joys and concerns experienced by the
faithful today. These experiences cannot be discerned in the
abstract, nor can they be identified solely by offices in Rome.
Instead, they can only be known by listening to the People of
God describe their sense of how the Spirit is speaking to them
and leading them. Therefore, in exploring the efforts to become a more synodal church, we cannot speak of synodality
solely in terms of its theological foundations, methods, and
transformative capacity. We must attend to the content of
what the People of God are saying. What follows are five

---

2. Ivereigh, "I Helped Write the First Global Synod Document."
3. Ivereigh, "I Helped Write the First Global Synod Document."

central themes shared by the People of God in the course of this unprecedented global consultation.

Theme #1: A Need for Formation

While the national reports reflect consensus on many subjects, perhaps the clearest and most dominant theme they voice is a desire for greater formation in terms of knowledge of the faith and synodal practices. The submission from Zimbabwe captures the prevalence of this appeal: "The thirst for formation runs through almost every synod submission."[4] This awareness of the Catholic faithful in Zimbabwe is shared by their fellow believers throughout the world. The People of God see formation as a basic and essential building block for a synodal church. Many noted that the faithful do not have an adequate sense of the faith and that a "lack of knowledge and formation keeps people from having confidence and hinders participation."[5] Also contained in these reports is the observation that "a lack of deep knowledge and scarcity of substantial faith reduces the laity's performance to liturgical and a few other undertakings in the church. Basically, people feel ill-equipped to respond to the call to evangelise."[6] This leaves some with the "misconception that priests and the consecrated have to do it all while they occupy the backbenches."[7]

The yearning for formation is not limited to a desire for knowledge but includes a desire for greater formation in synodal practices, habits, and means of participation. In particular,

---

4. Zimbabwe Catholic Bishops' Conference (ZCBC), National Synthesis Document, https://catholicchurchnewszimbabwe.blog/zimbabwe-catholic-bishops-conference-national-synthesis-document/.

5. Kenyan Conference of Catholic Bishops (KCCB), National Synod Report.

6. ZCBC, National Synthesis Document.

7. ZCBC, National Synthesis Document.

many submissions note that ecclesial communities need to be formed in the practices of communal discernment and shared decision-making. Here again, the church in Zimbabwe speaks for many: "We do not know how to discern well together. We are not yet a discerning Church, a Church able to identify the work of the Holy Spirit among us and follow its lead."[8]

A "thirst for formation" persists throughout the reports from around the world because formation is widely understood as critical to advancing many aspects of the church's life. The People of God identified many fruits that formation bears for the church's health. Formation stimulates participation inasmuch as properly formed leaders can invite and equip community members to participate more fully. It promotes greater accountability and transparency as people better understand the needs, roles, and responsibilities that exist among the faithful. It cultivates evangelization by instilling people with wisdom and language that fortifies their understanding of their faith and their ability to express it. Formation enables parents to be the first teachers of faith for the children, a role for which many are currently unequipped. Lastly, formation not only transmits knowledge, but it also instills zeal, outreach, and joy that, in turn, fosters unity and communion in the church. Around the world, the People of God see formation as a leaven that enlivens synodality in every part of the church's life.

Amidst the broad calls for formation, the People of God articulated a particular desire for bishops and clergy to receive more training. The faithful observed that ordained ministers step into important roles but do not always possess adequate preparation or necessary ongoing support. Priests and bishops often feel isolated and unsure about how to handle complicated theological questions and crises requiring pastoral responses. Many suggested that a critical step is a renewal of

---

8. ZCBC, National Synthesis Document.

seminary formation. This view is captured in the *Instrumentum Laboris* 2023 which states, "Candidates for ordained ministry must be trained in a synodal style and mentality. The promotion of a culture of synodality implies the renewal of the current seminary curriculum and the formation of teachers and professors of theology, so that there is a clearer and more decisive orientation towards formation for a life of communion, mission and participation." The text captures the essence of the People of God's comments on the thirst for greater formation: "Formation for a more genuinely synodal spirituality is at the heart of the renewal of the Church."[9]

Understanding what the listening church heard requires that we pay special attention to the Synthesis Report 2023, A Synodal Church in Motion, as this text not only brings together reports from multiple stages of consultation, but it also includes the fruits of the deep listening of those gathered at the round tables of the synod's general assembly. This document affirms formation as a primary theme voiced by the People of God; indeed, the topic is mentioned fifty-six times in its forty pages. It notes that the calls for formation echoed around the world should come as no surprise; Jesus himself underscored the importance of formation by devoting extensive time to forming his disciples.[10] Culminating all that was shared at various levels, the report states, "Formation in a synodal key is meant to enable the People of God to live out their baptismal vocation fully, in the family, in the workplace, in ecclesial, social, and intellectual spheres. It is meant to enable each person to participate actively in the Church's mission according to his or her own charisms and vocation."[11] Ultimately, throughout the synod process, the faithful around the world identify formation as a top priority for a synodal church.

9. *Instrumentum Laboris* 2023, 59.
10. Synthesis Report 2023, III. 14. a.
11. Synthesis Report 2023, III. 14. f.

Theme #2: A Desire for the Church to Be More Welcoming and Inclusive

A second clear and consistent theme expressed by the People of God is the desire for the church to be more welcoming and inclusive. Voices from every part of the world attest that the Holy Spirit is calling the church to be a community with open doors. The national report from the United States captures the deep desire for inclusion that is chorused throughout the world: "The most common desire named in the synodal consultations was to be a more welcoming church where all members of the People of God can find accompaniment on the journey."[12] The People of God in Zimbabwe affirm this desire, identifying a welcoming and inclusive church as the "dream" of the faithful. Their report remarks, "Largely, what emerges from the fruits, seeds and weeds of synodality are voices that have great love for the Church, voices that dream of a Church of credible witnesses, a Church that is inclusive, open and welcoming Family of God."[13] Throughout the world, the People of God communicate that an evangelizing church welcomes and calls everyone into shared life. They see this as unmistakably rooted in the ministry of Jesus, who was not afraid to break boundaries in his efforts to reach out to those on the margins. Together, the faithful on each continent envision a church that is "a home for the wounded and broken, not an institution for the perfect. They want the Church to meet people . . . wherever they are, and walk with them rather than judging them; to build real relationships through care and authenticity, not superiority."[14]

12. United States Conference of Catholic Bishops (USCCB), National Synthesis of the People of God in the United States of America for the Diocesan Phase of the 2021–23 Synod, 7, https://www.usccb.org/resources/US%20National%20Synthesis%202021-2023%20Synod.pdf.

13. ZCBC, National Synthesis Document.

14. USCCB, National Synthesis of the People of God, 7–8.

Reports from every corner of the globe bemoan the way that a lack of welcoming by the church causes wounds of exclusion, diminishes the community, and unnecessarily separates people from the church's sacramental life. They express a desire to enter into dialogue with those who feel a tension between belonging to the church and their loving relationships or their state of life. Submissions often identify groups who are excluded with regularity and to whom they wish to extend radical hospitality. These groups are not spoken of as "issues" or abstract statistics; reports speak of family members, neighbors, and children of God. In that sense the reports recognize a real and existing closeness that is challenged or wounded by a lack of ecclesial hospitality. Many voices call for inclusion of the poor, members of the LGBTQ+ community, people with physical or mental disabilities, people in irregular marriages, single mothers, and divorced people and their children. Some voices, especially those of young adults, confide that they are unsure that they can remain in a church that engages in practices they consider discriminatory. Others argue that a pattern of exclusion deepens the gulf between the church and the rest of society making it harder to share the Gospel.

While there is a clear call for the church to include everyone—or, in the words of Francis, "*todos, todos, todos*"[15]—there is a particular desire to create a sense of belonging for young people. The Asian continental report observes that while young people constitute 65 percent of the population on that continent, "they are relatively absent in the life of the

---

15. See, for example, Christopher White, "Pope Doubles Down on Message That Church Is Open to All, including LGBTQ People and Women," *National Catholic Register*, August 6, 2023, https://www.ncronline.org /vatican/vatican-news/pope-doubles-down-message-church-open-all -including-lgbtq-people-and-women.

Church."[16] Many communities around the globe speak about the ache caused by this absence. Families who have done all that they can to raise their children in the Catholic Church feel confused and even devastated when their children walk away from the faith that has been a source of comfort, sustenance, and identity for generations. Grandparents and parents cry out to the church to do more to engage their children and grandchildren. The Asian continental report states, "Amid the generational gap between the old and the young, the Church as a 'mother' needs to extend her loving embrace around the youth and reach out to those who are lost, confused, and have disconnected themselves from the Church. Though the reports state the youth are missing in the Church, perhaps a point to ponder is that the youth are possibly saying that the Church is missing in their lives."[17]

The calls for greater inclusion voiced in the national and continental reports do not focus on changing teachings or structures. Instead, they call the church to adopt a posture of openness and to develop effective modes of accompaniment. Communities around the world ask for guidance on how to minister to those who feel excluded by the church, guidance that can be applied immediately even while the church continues to discern its formal teachings. The US report makes an emotional plea in this regard, noting, "There is an urgent need for guidance as [one parish] begged, 'we believe that we are approaching a real crisis in how to minister to the LGBTQ+ community, some of whom are members of our own families. We need help, support and clarity.' " The lack of effective pastoral strategies contributes to a situation in which "families

16. Federation of Asian Bishops' Conferences, *Final Document of the Asian Continental Assembly on Synodality* 98, https://www.synodresources.org/resource_post/251850/.

17. Federation of Asian Bishops' Conferences, *Final Document of the Asian Continental Assembly on Synodality* 99.

'feel torn between remaining in the church and supporting their loved ones.'"[18]

The Synthesis Report, in a truly synodal style, offers back to local churches what it heard on the topic of inclusion in the form of a question: "What would need to change in order for those who feel excluded to experience the Church as more welcoming?"[19] It is careful to note that the change cannot come only in terms of enhanced listening and openness, but must also be manifest in actions. The commitment to becoming a more inclusive community must be translated into the church's practices, operational structures, means of pastoral outreach, and spiritual accompaniment. At every stage of the synodal process, the faithful around the world spoke a message in one voice: we want to be a welcoming church.

Theme #3: A New Style of Being Church and a New Style of Leadership

The global reports affirm an international awareness that synodality is central to the church's true nature. Voices on every continent express gratitude for the synod and a sense that it provides a dialogical, participatory, and, ultimately, authentic style of being church. The People of God in Nigeria effused, "The Synod has been a refreshing moment which thrilled most especially the laity, to see that they have a voice in the affairs of the Church and, together with their pastors, form one flock under the fold of Jesus the Good Shepherd. We hope that the enthusiasm experienced at this stage of our synodal conversations may be sustained so that it truly becomes our way."[20] Participants in listening sessions expressed

18. USCCB, *National Synthesis of the People of God*, 8.
19. *Synthesis Report 2023*, 16.n.
20. Catholic Bishops' Conference of Nigeria (CBCN), *National Synthesis Report for Nigeria*.

gratitude for being introduced to the method of spiritual conversation. Many commented that they see this method as illumining a way beyond the polarization that has become entrenched in their communities. Individuals expressed thanks for being asked to speak and being heard without interruption, apology, or judgment. They also appreciated the graced opportunity to listen to others, including those with diverse perspectives, and thereby come to know the church's life in new ways. The United States speaks for many in articulating that "the rediscovery of listening as basic posture of a church called to ongoing conversion is one of the most valuable gifts of the synodal experience in the United States."[21]

The reports also called for a transformation of leadership styles in the mode of synodality. Almost every report testifies to the prevalence of clericalism, understood as "negative or authoritarian attitudes among the clergy [that] inhibit listening, participation and communion."[22] From every corner of the church, people lamented leaders who embrace monarchical styles, isolate themselves from the community, abuse power, and exercise authority in a transactional manner. These experiences of authority suggested to many that "the Church seems to prioritize doctrine over people, rules and regulations over lived reality."[23] Several countries note that the crisis of trust in ecclesial authority brought about by clericalism has been deepened in recent decades in the wake of scandals related to clergy sexual abuse, residential boarding schools, and financial fraud. Namibia articulated a view that is widely held: "We need to reconsider our style of being church. Move away from judgmental and legalistic attitudes and move to greater humility, mercy, empathy and knowledge of Christ's

21. USCCB, National Synthesis of the People of God, 12.
22. Uganda Episcopal Conference (UEC), Synthesis Report of the Uganda Episcopal Conference.
23. USCCB, National Synthesis of the People of God, 7.

teachings and style. We need to show a 'less legalistic face of Christ.' "[24] While the reports are sharp in their critiques of clericalism, they also include positive ideas for moving forward. They express "a deep and energetic desire for renewed forms of leadership—priestly, episcopal, religious and lay—that are relational and collaborative, and forms of authority capable of generating solidarity and co-responsibility."[25] The People of God universally express a desire for shepherds who "smell like their sheep."

A growing appreciation for synodality brings with it a desire to cultivate a "spirituality of synodality." Communities around the world believe that such a spirituality is needed because the formal synod process cannot resolve every issue, nor is it intended to do so. Rather, the church needs to cultivate a spirituality of synodality so that it can navigate contemporary and future challenges. This is voiced in the Nigerian report, which confirms that "what is of primary importance is not that the People of God receive more information, but that they develop a spirituality of listening, accompaniment and attentiveness to the Spirit."[26] Such a spirituality is necessary not only because it supports decision-making but also because it promotes a shift from individual thinking to collective thinking. A spirituality of synodality is a spirituality of "we."[27]

The Synthesis Report underscores the global consensus around the church's synodal nature in its opening section, entitled "Synodality: Experience and Understanding." It begins by affirming that people around the world have found joy in a heightened awareness of the synodal dimension of the church. The report recalls that Scripture and tradition attest to synodal practice, even as communities adopted diverse forms at various

24. Namibia Catholic Bishops' Conference (NCBC), Synthesis Report.
25. Document for the Continental Stage 59.
26. CBCN, National Synthesis Report for Nigeria.
27. Document for the Continental Stage 85.

times. According to the report, the synodal journey has re-newed an "experience of and desire for the Church as God's home and family, a Church that is closer to the lives of Her people, less bureaucratic and more relational."[28] In this way, ecclesial synodality is essential to the future of the church. There can be no going back from the synodal path.

Theme #4: The Centrality of the Liturgy

The faithful around the globe chorused their sense that the liturgy stands as central to their experience and love of church. Throughout the synodal consultations, the faithful testified to the importance of dynamic, Christ-centered liturgies that gather and nourish people. A representative report stated, "The liturgical and sacramental life of the Church, particularly the centrality of the Eucharist, came up continually in all the dioceses as a point of unity, essential to Catholic identity, community, and a life of faith. Participants expressed a deep desire and hunger for God." The submission continues, "While perspectives differed on what constitutes 'good liturgy' and what areas need renewal or better understanding, there was universal agreement on the significance of the Eucharist in the life of the Church."[29]

On the topic of liturgy, a concern raised by almost every country was the need for better homilies. The People of God asked that greater effort be directed by clergy at preparing homilies that are thoughtful, relevant, rooted in the Scripture readings, and inspiring. Enlarge the Space of Your Tent ad-dresses the matter bluntly: "The quality of homilies is almost unanimously reported as a problem: there is a call for 'deeper homilies, centered on the Gospel and the readings of the day,

---

28. Synthesis Report 2023, 1b.
29. USCCB, National Synthesis of the People of God, 7.

and not on politics, making use of accessible and attractive language that refers to the lives of the faithful.' "[30]

Another prominent concern was the lack of lay participation. Voices around the world lamented the way that liturgies are often too focused on the celebrant and view the laity as passive participants. Appeals to create more active roles for the laity, like one made by Ethiopia, came with frequency: "While being faithful to the tradition, its originality, antiquity, and uniformity, let us try to make the liturgical celebration more alive and participatory of all the community of believers; priests, laity, youth and children, reading the signs of the time with sound discernment. The young people are trying to have a space in the liturgy with songs and it is positive."[31]

While many reports underscore people's experience of the liturgy as the "source and summit" of the church's life and a focal point for its unity, several remarked on the unfortunate ways that it can serve as a point of division. Some comments focused on the way that debates over liturgy promote internal fragmentation, while others focused on how the liturgy can reflect, and even deepen, divides between the church and the wider culture. Regarding internal divisions, many of the faithful noted that disagreements about liturgical practices typically grow out of larger theological disagreements about the church. The European Continental Assembly confirms, "The liturgical dimension in the Church is a place of strong tensions. These tensions are part of a deeper tension of an ecclesiological

---

30. Document for the Continental Stage 93. The internal quotation comes from the report submitted by the Maronite Church. The problem of weak preaching was already signaled during the Synod on the Eucharist (2005) and Synod on the Word of God (2008) and led to extensive comments on preaching by Pope Francis in *Evangelii Gaudium* (2013) and the publication of a Homiletic Directory by the Vatican's Congregation for Divine Worship and the Discipline of the Sacraments (2014).

31. Document for the Continental Stage 91.

nature. Ecclesiological tension often arises from a vision of the Church based on one's own expectations."[32] Catholics in the United States recorded, "Sadly, celebration of the Eucharist is also experienced as an area of division within the church. The most common issue regarding the liturgy is the celebration of the pre-Conciliar Mass."[33] They also shared that differences over how to celebrate the liturgy "sometimes reach the level of animosity. People on each side of the issue reported feeling judged by those who differ from them."[34]

The People of God also note that liturgy exists as a flashpoint in the church's struggle to speak meaningfully within modern cultures. They recognize that communal worship is a space where the church's struggle to balance its distinctive identity with a need to read the signs of the times becomes particularly clear and public. Anxieties about this tension were especially pronounced in submissions from European countries that worry that the distance between the church and secular culture is on the brink of becoming unbridgeable. Representatives from the Nordic countries affirm this saying, "The gap . . . between tradition and modernity is becoming increasingly wide and more and more aggressive. This is particularly painful in the area of liturgy (Nordic countries). Indeed, for liturgy—and not only liturgy—it is important to use a language that adheres to tradition while being significant for the people of our time."[35]

The faithful from countries in other parts of the world spoke about the relationship between liturgy and culture in terms of the need for greater inculturation. They want to ex-

---

32. Catholic Conference of European Bishops (CCEE), Final Dossier for the European Continental Assembly, 67, https://www.ccee.eu/wp-content/uploads/sites/2/2023/04/Documento-finale-Praga-Prague-final-document-online_DEF.pdf.
33. USCCB, National Synthesis of the People of God, 5.
34. USCCB, National Synthesis of the People of God, 5.
35. CCEE, Final Dossier for the European Continental Assembly, 62.

perience the church "with a local face."[36] They call the church to better recognize, engage, integrate, and respond to the richness of local cultures and incorporate this richness into the liturgy. To achieve this integration, they ask that liturgical texts and resources be made available in local languages, that the faithful have more opportunities to share and contribute in their native tongue, and that liturgical questions be addressed from perspectives beyond that of Europe. The faithful point out that recognizing a diversity of liturgical practices would be an exercise in synodal hospitality and provide a better witness to the Gospel.

A Synodal Church in Motion shows a maturity, gained by the experience of journeying together, in speaking about the connection between liturgy and synodality. In particular, it speaks of the power of liturgy to form people in their faith and in synodal practices. This is because "liturgy celebrated with authenticity is the first and fundamental school of discipleship."[37] In this synodal journey, we have learned that synodality is deeply liturgical and liturgy is deeply synodal. This fuels calls from around the world for the church to re-center its life on the liturgy and to create vibrant liturgies that sustain and animate the synodal journey.

Theme #5: Women

A final theme woven throughout the synodal reports is the need to rethink women's participation in the church. Enlarge the Space of Your Tent attests that the issue of women's roles "registered all over the world" and that "almost all reports raise the issue of full and equal participation of women."[38] It

---

36. Catholic Bishops' Conference of Ethiopia (CBCE), National Synod Report, 8.

37. Synthesis Report 2023, 3k.

38. Document for the Continental Stage 60, 64.

observes that every continent includes "an appeal for Catholic women to be valued first and foremost as baptised and equal members of the People of God."[39] The call to renew women's roles represents an example of the church hearing something new by expanding how it listened. To be clear, concerns about women's roles in the church are not new, but what is new is that this issue has never been identified as a global concern. Catholics in North America and Europe have often been told that their calls for expanded and empowered roles for women are a myopic concern of the West, something that Catholics in Asia or Africa are not talking about. Yet the reports from local churches across the globe testify to the fact that the need to elevate the status of women is a conversation being had by Catholics all over the world. This includes the topic of ordination to the diaconate and/or priesthood.

Across cultural contexts, the reports conveyed that, even in the roles that are available to women, too often they are not taken seriously. Many remark that the unequal treatment of women is especially striking given the fact that they are the majority of those who attend liturgies, participate in church activities, and increasingly work in pastoral or support roles. The Holy Land report states, "In a Church where almost all decision-makers are men, there are few spaces where women can make their voices heard. Yet they are the backbone of Church communities, both because they represent the majority of the practising members and because they are among the most active members of the Church."[40] The Korean report confirms: "Despite the great participation of women in various Church activities, they are often excluded from key decision-making processes. Therefore, the Church needs to improve its awareness and institutional aspects of their activities."[41]

39. Document for the Continental Stage 61.
40. Document for the Continental Stage 61.
41. Document for the Continental Stage 61.

One of the starkest assessments of the status of women in the church comes in a report submitted by the Superiors of Institutes of Consecrated Life. In detailing discrimination faced by women religious, it notes that "sexism in decision-making and Church language is prevalent in the Church. . . . As a result, women are excluded from meaningful roles in the life of the Church, discriminated against by not receiving a fair wage for their ministries and services. Women religious are often regarded as cheap labour."[42]

The reports note that barring women from authoritative roles and excluding them from decision-making tables deprives the church of the perspectives and contributions of over half the members of our community. This failure not only impoverishes the ecclesial community, but it presents a "stumbling block for the Church in the modern world."[43] Further, the People of God insist that women, who represent over half of the global population, cannot be referred to monolithically, as if they represent one group. Women are united in faith, baptismal dignity, and love of the church, but they are also incredibly diverse. In fact, one of the only ways that all women are the same is that they are restricted from many leadership roles in the church. It is because women have often been "relegated to a prophetic edge" that they have much to offer the synod's efforts to transform the church.[44]

Submissions to the synod also lament the discrimination faced by women in spheres outside of the church. Women often do not receive fair pay, equal respect, or just treatment in their communities and their places of employment. They are hindered by gaps in education, wages, training, and expectations regarding childcare. Across the world, the faithful call out for the church to work to close these gaps. In a powerful

42. Document for the Continental Stage 63.
43. Document for the Continental Stage 62.
44. Document for the Continental Stage 61.

passage, Enlarge the Space of Your Tent expresses the cries of women who reach out to the church for assistance: "In every area of their lives, women ask the Church to be their ally. This includes addressing the social realities of impoverishment, violence and diminishment faced by women across the globe. They call for a Church at their side, and greater understanding and support in combating these forces of destruction and exclusion. Women participating in the synodal processes desire both Church and society to be a place of flourishing, active participation and healthy belonging."[45]

People raised their voices in the synod reports to confess many "uncomfortable truths" about women's status in the church and in society, in the hopes of pursuing conversion.[46] The faithful conveyed that many of their hopes for the church are inextricably connected to changes in women's roles. The world church is undivided in its sense that elevating the status of women is connected to changing the church's culture in a way that would inevitably make it more authentically itself and more synodal.

The Synthesis Report foregrounds the roles and dignity of women as central in what the Holy Spirit is saying to the church. Members of the synod assembly reflected on their own experience: "We have had a very positive experience of the reciprocity between women and men during this Assembly. Together we echo the call made in the previous phases of the synodal process, that the Church adopt a more decisive commitment to understand and accompany women from a pastoral and sacramental point of view."[47] Here again the text offers back to the local churches what it heard in the form of a question. It asks, "In order to give better expression to the gifts and charisms of all and to be more responsive to pastoral needs, how can the Church include more women in existing

---

45. Document for the Continental Stage 62.
46. Reynolds, "Are We Protagonists Yet?"
47. Synthesis Report 2023, 9.c.

roles and ministries?" Churches across the globe conveyed with unanimity that they want the contributions of women to be recognized and valued, and they want women to have more opportunities to exercise pastoral leadership.

Conclusion

The themes identified above provide a sense of what the People of God shared during the Synod on Synodality's multi-year, multi-phase consultation. As invited, the faithful spoke with *parrhesia* about their sense of where the Holy Spirit is calling the church. Their responses reflect a range of distinctive experiences and contexts. They also reflect a high level of agreement about the way the Holy Spirit is moving within the church and leading the People of God. We hear the faithful call out for more formation, greater inclusion, an embrace of synodal structures and practices, better liturgies, and new roles for women. The dreams and frustrations conveyed in the reports demand our earnest attention as the church seeks to move forward together. They help the church to move and grow in directions that are faithful to the promptings of God.

The themes which emerged around the world also illumine the style of synodality as an ongoing communal journey. While the faithful boldly name their desires, they do not insist on particular ways to achieve them. For example, the People of God are unanimous in wanting an inclusive church, but they do not insist on the means for achieving this goal. The synodal reports at every level avoid presenting their views in a prescriptive manner. The rhetoric of the submissions is not adversarial; that would not be a fruit of the Spirit. Instead, the reports show genuine inquiry and shared searching. This reflects the fact that, as Timothy Radcliffe stated so well, the work of the synod is "more like planting a tree than winning a battle."[48] For

---

48. Radcliffe, *Listening Together*, 116.

while we may not yet have arrived at shared conclusions, "we have begun to share the same questions."[49] Ultimately these themes expose not just what the People of God said but how a synodal church might advance toward that horizon.

These themes are best read with a spirit of hope that the church can live as a more authentic version of itself. In his retreat for synod participants ahead of the general assembly in October of 2023, Radcliffe explored the role of hope in the synodal journey. He noted, "We gather in hope for the church and for humanity. But here is the difficulty: we have contradictory hopes! So how can we hope together?"[50] Radcliffe insists that a key purpose of the synod is realized in "hoping together." Achieving this requires expanding the horizon of our hope, and that unfolds through mutual listening. The synod does not just offer a commitment to listening or a method of listening; it involves concrete acts of listening and subsequent acting on what was heard. In hearing the experiences and concerns of the People of God around the world, we learn to hope beyond our preconceived aspirations and to include the dreams of others. Radcliffe tells us, "If we listen to the Lord and to each other, seeking to understand his will for the church and the world, we shall be united in a hope that transcends our disagreements and be touched by the one whom St. Augustine called that 'beauty so ancient and so new . . . I tasted you and now hunger and thirst for you, you touched me, and I have burned for your peace.'"[51]

49. Radcliffe, *Listening Together*, 136.
50. Radcliffe, *Listening Together*, 7.
51. Radcliffe, *Listening Together*, 14.

Part II

Synodalizing the Church

How We Move Forward from Here

Chapter Five

What Does It Take to Synodalize the Church?

In part one (chapters one through four), we explored the journey so far: foundational theological concepts, historical roots, concrete snapshots, and emerging topics. While the Synod 2021–24 played a major role in helping the church to be more synodal, it has also become clear that synodality is something much larger; we are not done yet! Pope Francis has articulated the conviction that synodality needs to become an all-pervasive "constitutional" dimension of the church. The theologian Rafael Luciani speaks of a "synodalization" of the entire church.[1] Here in part two, we explore what it will take to grow in journeying together in an inclusive, participative, and discerning spirit. How to synodalize the church?

Before we make specific proposals, this chapter looks into the *elements* that are needed for such a transformation. We will highlight three that are essential for synodalizing the church: proper attitudes and behavior, appropriate structures, and meaningful practices. Attitudes and behavior require a personal commitment and include, for example, listening well; they address the subjective dimension. Structures are more

---

1. Luciani, *Synodality*, 70.

objective, including, for example, procedures for joint deci-sion-making. With the word *practices* we mean sets of habits and customs that typically situate themselves in between the subjective and the objective.

The underlying issue is change; therefore, we will start the chapter with this topic. The call for synodalizing attitudes and behaviors, structures, and practices implies that renewal and reform are appreciated as an essential and normal dimension of ecclesial life. Evidently and importantly, the changes we propose are not random. Attitudes, structures, and practices make no sense when they are viewed apart from the theo-logical commitments that they are meant to express. Develop-ment, renewal, or reform should represent a more helpful, truthful, and salutary way of presenting, living, and organizing the faith. In other words, the objective and the measuring stick is always greater fidelity to the Gospel.

Renewal and Reform

The underlying issue of synodalizing the church is renewal and reform. The terms overlap, with renewal evoking espe-cially inward, personal change, and reform addressing outward, ecclesial-structural change.[2] The latter term makes us think of the axiom *Ecclesia semper reformanda*: the church must always be in the process of reform. Often attributed to Saint Augustine, the phrase conveys the belief that renewal belongs to the very essence of the church. History warrants this fact. As we have seen in chapter two, the first generation of Chris-tians lived through a major transformation of faith practices and faith convictions. Renewal and reform are important for at least two reasons. First, human interpretations of the faith and human behavior are prone to misunderstandings and sin;

---

2. For a detailed terminological discussion, see Peter de Mey, "Church Renewal and Reform in the Documents of Vatican II: History, Theology, Terminology," *The Jurist* 71 (2011): 369–400.

renewal and reform are our way out of that. Second, faith is lived in ever-changing circumstances. A perpetual need for renewal and reform exists because church life seeks to live out faith in concrete times and places.

Unfortunately, the word *reform* took on something of a negative connotation in the Catholic Church in the wake of the Protestant Reformation. In the early modern period, the notion of reform became increasingly associated with those who disagreed with, and ultimately separated themselves from, the Roman church. Many reformers sought significant doctrinal and pastoral change; the church's defensive response tended to characterize change as unnecessary and even dangerous, since it saw itself as enjoying divine guidance and possessing unassailable teachings. Thus, for a long time, most voices within Catholicism viewed the idea of church reform negatively and regarded it as something reserved for an emergency situation. Reform pointed to failures that needed to be repaired rather than ongoing growth in ecclesial holiness and conforming the church to God's divine life.

This mentality began to shift at the time of Vatican II, as the council retrieved an ancient notion of reform as a positive and normal aspect of the church's life. Through its efforts to bring the church up to date (*aggiornamento*) by returning to its origins (*ressourcement*), Vatican II approached renewal and reform as a reality inherent to the church, part of a living tradition that must constantly grow and adapt in order to communicate its eternal message. Several historians at the council advocated this position by arguing that church history is resplendent with evidence of change and development. In fact, they argued that those who opposed reform and renewal lacked a sufficiently broad understanding of the church's own tradition.

As a result, the openings words of the very first document to be approved, the Constitution on the Sacred Liturgy, *Sacrosanctum Concilium*, highlight renewal as one of the objectives of the council and speak of adaptations to what "our age" needs: "The sacred council has set out . . . to adapt more closely to the needs of our age those institutions which are subject to change" (n. 1). The council is a historically situated event and must embrace its situatedness by renewal. Similarly, the Decree on Ecumenism, *Unitatis Redintegratio*, speaks of both renewal and reform—which was certainly an ecumenical gesture—as a way to remain faithful to Christ in changing circumstances:

> Every renewal [*renovatio*] of the church essentially consists in an increase of fidelity to her own calling. . . . Christ summons the church, as she goes on her pilgrim way, to that continual reformation [*reformatio*] of which she always has need, insofar as she is a human institution here on earth. Consequently, if, in various times and circumstances, there have been deficiencies in moral conduct or in church discipline, or even in the way that church teaching has been formulated—to be carefully distinguished from the deposit of faith itself—these should be set right at the opportune moment. (n. 6)

Vatican II's efforts to renew and reform the church retrieve the axiom *Ecclesia semper reformanda*. While each pontificate seeks to renew and reform in one form or another, arguably Pope Francis has gone about this task more boldly than his predecessors. Shortly after becoming pope, he stated in a homily: "*Ecclesia semper reformanda*. The Church always needs to be renewed since her members are sinners and continually need to be converted."[3] Here one can see Francis's close association between the life of the faithful and the nature of the church, which fuels his sense that ecclesial structures and ecclesial life stand in mutual relationship. Soon after, in *Evangelii Gaudium*, the idea of perennial reform emerged as a prominent theme. Francis shared his vision of reform by

---

3. Pope Francis, Morning Meditation, The Water Flowing through the Church, November 9, 2013, https://www.vatican.va/content/francesco/en/cotidie/2013/documents/papa-francesco-cotidie_20131109_water-flowing.html.

calling for a "pastoral and missionary conversion" of the church. In a critical passage, he noted, " 'I dream of a 'missionary option,' that is, a missionary impulse capable of transforming everything, so that the Church's customs, ways of doing things, times and schedules, language and structures can be suitably channeled for the evangelization of today's world rather than for her self-preservation" (EG 27). For Francis, the goal of ecclesial reform is not greater theological clarity or technical dogmatic precision, but it is about facilitating mission: how can the church be closer to where people are at and transform their lives with God's mercy? Genuine pastoral conversion implies an openness to renewal.

Importantly, this type of renewal is ongoing and outgoing. For Francis, a key aspect of ecclesial renewal is the idea of *motion*. A stagnant church, one that obsesses about its own self-preservation and devotes its time to "navel gazing," develops a false sense of its identity and generates structures inimical to spreading the Gospel. Francis regularly invokes motion-related language to speak about the ecclesial community. In *Evangelii Gaudium*, he offers his thoughts on ecclesial reform under the heading "A Church which goes forth" (EG 20). The text speaks of the church as "being sent out," "going to the peripheries," "taking a first step," and "always moving forward." *Outgoing* renewal comes with *ongoing* renewal. In a particularly memorable homily, Francis likened the church to a bicycle. He suggested that "the equilibrium of the church is like balancing a bicycle: it is stable and it goes well when it is moving. When you stop it, it falls." He further elaborated that a bicycle "stays upright as long as it keeps moving" and that "the equilibrium of the church is found precisely in its mobility."[4] Thus, for Francis the church is constituted by both centrifugal forces—forces which propel the

---

4. See "Pope Francis: The Church Is like a Bike—It Stays Up if It Keeps Moving," *America*, April 25, 2018, https://www.americamagazine.org /faith/2018/04/25/pope-francis-church-bike-it-stays-if-it-keeps-moving.

community of disciples outward in outreach—and centripetal forces—forces which draw God's people and all of creation into communion. Communion and mission are complementary dimensions of the church. They both require ongoing reform and renewal.

Attitudes and Behavior: Personal Conversion

Renewal and reform need to become real in attitudes and behavior, structures, and practices; they need incarnation. A first way of concretizing renewal is situated at the personal level and manifests itself in the form of human behavior. The importance of actions is very clear from the life of Jesus. The salvation he spoke about he also realized and embodied through acts of kindness, healing, liberation, nourishment, and service. Thus, Jesus' teaching became convincing by being incarnate—that is, being tangible and real.

Christians, too, are called to live their faith in an incarnate way. Indeed, the gospels contain a double invitation: to believe in Jesus and to follow Jesus through our actions. Parables like those of the Good Samaritan (Luke 10) and the Last Judgement (Matt 25) highlight the ultimate importance of behavior, in this case, serving the least of our brothers and sisters. The letter of James warns us that faith alone is not enough; we need to show our faith in what we actually do: "What good is it, my brothers and sisters, if you say you have faith but do not have works? Can faith save you? If a brother or sister is naked and lacks daily food, and one of you says to them, 'Go in peace; keep warm and eat your fill,' and yet you do not supply their bodily needs, what is the good of that? So faith by itself, if it has no works, is dead" (Jas 2:14-17).

Thus, our behavior—or "works"—articulates without words what we believe and makes the words we do speak convincing and real. Yet their significance is greater still, for deeds also fashion faith. That becomes clear by recalling the old liturgical adage *lex orandi lex credendi*. The dense Latin phrase means that our prayer (*lex orandi*) is our faith (*lex credendi*); the two mutually articulate and shape one another. Importantly, our prayer involves words, gestures, and other concrete elements. For example, the act of kneeling after receiving Communion speaks of our faith in God and fashions that faith. By kneeling we express our reverence for God and thus profess his greatness. Importantly, the axioms can also be inverted: how and what we believe suggests how and what to pray. One who believes that God cares for us might express this faith by joyfully singing the Taizé chant "*Bonum est confidere*" ("it is good to trust") and, in so doing, surrender to God's fatherly and motherly care.

One could enrich the adage by adding phrases such as *lex vivendi* and *lex congregandi*: the way we live our (faith) life and the way we gather, both liturgically and otherwise, articulate our faith and shape it.[5] To use the example of *lex credendi lex vivendi* (what we believe expresses and shapes how we live): if we imagine the church primarily as an organization, the fitting behavior is to obediently follow its rules. It also works the other way round: how we act says something about how we imagine the church and shapes that imagination. To use the same example: by being obedient, we live out (and thus build up) the notion of the church as a sacred organization. Yet by living out other virtues, we embody other ecclesiological convictions. For example, mutual listening builds up a different experience and a different ecclesiological imagination, namely, that of the church as a community in which we journey as companions—the People of God, in ecclesiological terms.

Thematizing attitudes and behavior is important, as official documents consider them the basis for synodalizing the church. Pope Francis insists that conversion has priority and

---

5. See Arnaud Join-Lambert, "Les liturgies synodales comme lieu ecclésiologique," *La Maison-Dieu* 287 (2017): 113–36, 114.

is wary of focusing too much on structural reforms; the latter follows from the former. Here the *Vademecum* speaks clearly: "The Synodal Process will naturally call for a renewal of structures at various levels of the church, in order to foster deeper communion, fuller participation, and more fruitful mission. At the same time, the experience of synodality should not focus first and foremost on structures, but on the experience of journeying together to discerning the path forward, inspired by the Holy Spirit. The conversion and renewal of structures will come about only through the on-going conversion and renewal of all the members of the Body of Christ."[6]

The German Carmelite theologian Michael Plattig points out that this corresponds with the experience of religious communities. These communities, Plattig says, generally agree that "communal processes need structures, but also attitudes [*Grundhaltungen*]; without the latter a synodal project very quickly fails."[7]

It is, therefore, unfortunate that the magisterium and professional theologians do not go into great depth regarding what attitudes one needs; they tend to focus on theory. This holds true in general and applies specifically to synodality also. Usually, the magisterium sees its task as protecting the orthodoxy of the faith content within the church. Less attention is given to practice, and if practice is attended to, it usually means a

6. General Secretariat for the Synod, *Vademecum* 2.4. While acknowledging the need for structural and canonical reform, the *Instrumentum Laboris* for the 2023 Synod also recalled that "the Continental Assemblies strongly expressed the conviction that structures alone are not enough, but that a change of mindset is also needed, hence the need to invest in formation" (B 3.3d). See also what the Synthesis Report states: "A profound spiritual conversion is needed as the foundation for any effective structural change" (9f).

7. Michael Plattig, OCarm, "Gehorsam: Grundhaltung für synodale Prozesse," in *Synodalisierung: Eine Zerreißprobe für die katholische Weltkirche? Expertinnen und Experten aus aller Welt beziehen Stellung*, ed. Paul Zulehner, Peter Neuner, and Anna Hennersperger (Ostfildern: Grünewald, 2022), 104.

narrow set of ethical issues. In the case of synodality, official documents on the synod speak of journeying and listening without spelling out how that works concretely, except for promoting the spiritual conversation method.

A similar tendency characterizes most professional theologians: they see it as their task to work towards greater faith insight, which they seek to achieve through historical considerations, textual criticism, psychology, philosophy, and so on. Here, too, much less attention is given to practice.[8] In the context of synodality also, theological literature is mainly theoretical, focusing on church history, canon law, and theological clarifications. Practical elements such as attitudes, behavior, and practices are much less considered.[9] For example, I (Jos) know of only a few recent in-depth treatments by theologians of the practice of listening in relation to synodality.[10]

The lack of interest in synodal attitudes, behavior, and practices is worrying in various regards. First, how can we become a synodal church without greater interest in the practice of

8. In recent years, "lived theology" has gained momentum as a way to do theology in dialogue with people's experience, but most theological disciplines are still on their way to integrating it.

9. See Jos Moons, SJ, "A Weakness Exposed: Theologians on the Practice of Synodality," in *Theology Responding to the Challenge of Synodality: Proceedings of International Conference Held at the Pontifical Gregorian University (Rome, 27–29 April 2023)*, ed. Nathalie Becquart, XMCJ, and Philipp Renczes, SJ (Rome: Libreria Editrice Vaticana, 2024), 463–70.

10. Plattig, "Gehorsam: Grundhaltung für synodale Prozesse." Cf. Elisa Estévez López and Nurya Martínez-Gayol Fernández, " 'Escuchar, dialogar y discernir' con las mujeres. Retos de una Iglesia sinodal," *Estudios Eclesiásticos: Revista trimestral de investigación e información teológica* 97 (2022): 555–89; Randall S. Rosenberg, "Cultivating a Synodal Disposition in Theological Education," in *Theology Responding to the Challenge of Synodality*, ed. Becquart and Renczes, 333–45; Stefan Silber, "Synodalität als ekklesiologisches Prinzip ad intra und ad extra: Lernen von der Bischofssynode für Amazonien," *Zeitschrift für Missionswissenschaft und Religionswissenschaft* 105 (2021): 34–47.

synodality? It is as if theologians think that insight automatically leads to action—which would be a naïve view of the functioning of human beings. Psychologists point out that our behavior is much less rational than we like to think and that many of our decisions are made at less conscious and unconscious levels.

Moreover, synodality is a *new* way of proceeding and therefore requires *new* attitudes (such as openness), *new* behavior (such as active listening), and *new* practices (such as common discernment) that do not come easy. For example, psychologists and spiritual directors know that listening is a complex art involving skills such as active listening; self-knowledge, so that one listens to the other person instead of to oneself; and an affective antenna that hears unspoken or half-spoken messages. As active listening and most other attitudes, behavior, and practices necessary for synodality are not common practice, it is sad that these aspects are usually not elaborated in magisterial teaching or theological reflection. How is the church supposed to practice synodal skills such as active listening if official documents and theological literature rarely speak of them?

Reforming Structures: Structural Conversion

In addition to personal conversion, synodalizing the church also involves its rules, procedures, and organizational levels—in short, structures. These structures are meant to cultivate order in the community and instantiate deep theological convictions such as the nature of membership in the Body of Christ, the meaning of God's redemptive plan, and the manner in which Christ and the Spirit dwell among us. In fact, however, church structures, understood juridically or as administrative constructs, can seem cold, technical, and focused on power. Aren't they far removed from, or even inimical, healthy relationships, our faith in Jesus Christ, and our efforts to live lives of discipleship?

Therefore, developing more synodal structures should start with renewing the appreciation of structures and institutions. A growing body of research observes increasing levels of anti-institutional bias in places like North America and Europe. Many of the governmental, educational, and religious institutions that have long enjoyed solid public trust have seen trust eroded at an alarming rate. For example, between the 1970s and 2022, a Gallup poll of US adults reported that individuals who indicated "a great deal" or "quite a lot" of confidence in the banking system declined from 60 percent to 27 percent, with similar numbers for confidence in the medical system (from 80 percent to 38 percent) and major US institutions.[11] The factors fueling this drop are hard to identify and weigh, but researchers point to major events such as the crash of the space shuttle Columbia (2003), failures in the response to Hurricane Katrina (2005), and the collapse of the financial system during the Great Recession (2008). Other factors include a growing perception that institutions lack transparency, tolerate corruption, and fail to honor shared social values.

The growing suspicion of institutions impact how people view the church. While the church's own actions have certainly contributed to the breakdown in confidence it has experienced, this erosion must be seen within this wider trend. In his "last lecture," noted ecclesiologist Richard Gaillardetz warned us that we should withstand the temptation to do away with the institutional dimension of the church:

> In the face of this widespread cultural distrust of institutions and the understandable disillusionment of many Catholics with the Church's institutional failings, it is all

---

11. Jeffrey M. Jones, "Confidence in U.S. Institutions Down; Average at New Low," *Gallup Poll*, July 5, 2022; and Gallup Poll cited in Springtide Research Institute, *The State of Religion & Young People: Relational Authority; Catholic Edition* (Farmington, MN: Springtide Research Institute), 32.

the more important that we avoid any romantic pining for a church set free from the constraints of institutional reality. After all, institutions, when functioning well, are but a spatial and temporal extension of the fundamentally social character of human nature. Certainly, we must not reduce the church to its institutional dimension, but any sweeping dismissal of the institutional life of the church in service of church reform is both misguided and doomed to failure.[12]

In the case of the church, appreciating structures means appreciating *hierarchical* structures. In the modern world, and perhaps especially in democratic countries, structures that reflect a "hierarchy" of authority receive particular skepticism. For many, the notion of hierarchy evokes negative images of powerful people trying to usurp the liberty and self-expression of those who have less power. Over against that deformed and misconceived notion of hierarchy, its true purpose is to provide order so that the entire community can flourish. Without order—when chaos reigns—it is impossible for every member of the community to develop and share her/his/their gifts, and for the group as a whole to reach its full potential. Therefore, rather than seeking to stifle individual self-expression and distinctiveness, ecclesial hierarchy and structures, when they are at their best, promote the functioning of the church as a social body and allow for community and diversity.

However, that has not always been the case. We should admit that the hierarchical trait of the church can be, and has been, deformed into a culture of clericalism and that some structures obstruct synodality and therefore need reform. The Synthesis Report 2023 defined clericalism as "a misunderstanding of the divine call, viewing it more as a privilege than a service, and

---

12. Richard Gaillardetz, "Loving and Reforming a Holy yet Broken Church: My Last Lecture," *Worship* 97 (2023): 66.

manifesting itself . . . in a worldly manner that refuses to allow itself to be accountable."[13] Pope Francis has directed some of his harshest critiques towards clericalism. He has denounced it as, in Fr. Radcliffe's words, "the curse that poisons our encounter with each other and with God, the utter negation of synodality."[14] Addressing the synod participants in October 2023, Francis said, "Clericalism is a scourge, it is a blow. It is a form of worldliness that defiles and damages the face of the Lord's bride; it enslaves the holy, faithful people of God."[15]

The remedy for clericalism is for leaders to understand themselves as fellow pilgrims within the People of God and to see one's leadership role—be it an ordained or other role—as one of service within that body.[16] Importantly, that is how many deacons, priests, and bishops already operate: as servant leaders. To leave behind a clerical mentality, we need to look towards the laity, too. Members of the laity promote a clerical culture when they passively defer all work in the church to bishops and priests, or when they exercise their own leadership in the church at the expense of empowering and accompanying others.

However, more is needed than a personal conversion of mentality and behavior. As some ecclesial structures promote clerical thinking and clerical ways of proceeding, structures, too, need to be reformed. For example, experts in canon law point out that the Code of Canon Law needs rebalancing, for in its current form it is more concerned about the authority of the bishop than about the participation of all. Myriam Wijlens,

13. Synthesis Report 2023, 11c.

14. Radcliffe, *Listening Together*, 128.

15. Pope Francis, Intervention of the Holy Father at the 18th General Congregation of the 16th Ordinary General Assembly of the Synod of Bishops, October 25, 2023, https://www.vatican.va/content/francesco/en/speeches/2023/october/documents/20231025-intervento-sinodo.html.

16. In 2015, Pope Francis argued that hierarchical leadership should be understood within the framework of synodality, not above it: Pope Francis, Ceremony Commemorating the 50th Anniversary.

a senior advisor to the Synod Secretariat, observes that canon law specifies the ways in which the faithful have to obey or submit to the magisterium when it exercises its teaching office "without at the same time making any provision for an obligation on the side of the bishops to ascertain the *sensus fidei fidelium.*"[17] Similarly, Canadian canon lawyer Chad Glendinning points out that the Code places the functioning of diocesan synods wholly in the hands of the bishop, which is unfortunate, as such synods are meant to include the voice and vision of all. Glendinning writes that under current law the bishop "convokes [the diocesan synod], determines its agenda, presides over it, and dissolves or suspends it. The diocesan bishop alone 'signs the synodal declarations and decrees, which can be published by his authority alone' (can. 466)."[18]

Finally, it is certainly helpful to acknowledge that an authentic notion of human freedom can reorient perceptions about ecclesial structures. In today's world, people typically see freedom as unrestricted freedom of choice. In such a framework, it appears that "maximal choices = maximal freedom." Accordingly, anything that reduces one's options, including structures, is seen as a violation of freedom and an affront to personal dignity. However, in the theological tradition, freedom and restrictions are not opposed; instead, freedom consists in freely embracing and creatively living one's vocation. Ultimately,

17. Myriam Wijlens, " 'The Church of God Is Convoked in Synod': Theological and Canonical Challenges Concerning the 2021–2023 Synod," *Centro Pro Unione Semi-Annual Bulletin* 100 (2021): 92. This example and the next one are taken from Jos Moons and Robert Alvarez, *Theological Briefing Papers for the Synod 2023*, https://www.synodresources.org/newsletter_post/theological-briefing-papers-for-the-synod-assembly-2023/, Paper 2: Participation, the People of God, and the *Sensus Fidelium*, and Paper 4: Canon Law and Structures for Synodality.

18. Chad J. Glendinning, "Structures of Accountability in the Parish and Diocese: Lessons Learned in North America and Possibilities for Reform," *Studia Canonica* 56 (2022): 652.

freedom, in the theological tradition, entails freely relinquishing certain choices so that human beings may become their most authentic selves, rooted in divine vocation.

Two examples may illustrate the true nature of freedom. First, when a person chooses to get married, she or he commits solely to another person and forsakes the possibility of entering into romantic relationships with anybody else. So it can be said that this person is "less free." Yet, in a theological sense, this person actually experiences the freedom of living out one's vocation of a loving and supportive relationship. Similarly, in having children, parents limit the ways they're able to spend their time in many ways. Spending their evenings giving baths and reading stories rather than going out to a movie, a restaurant, or a friend's house seems like a restriction of freedom. Rather than weekend getaways, Saturdays are dominated by soccer schedules, playdates, and birthday parties. Yet in committing themselves to parenthood and entering into the depths of a parent-child relationship, as well as new depths of the relationship with their spouse, many people find themselves to be most fulfilled and most free to be who they were meant to be.

While the previous example challenges the idea that commitments—and the restrictions they imply—makes one unhappy, a second example challenges the idea that living according to a predetermined structure makes one unhappy. This example comes from religious life. I (Kristin) teach at a Benedictine college associated with a large abbey of over one hundred monks. In addition to limited freedom—these men usually do not have bank accounts, do not own cars, and do not choose what they will have for dinner—their lives are highly structured. Community members wake up early almost every day of the year for morning prayer and drop whatever they are doing several times a day when the bells of the abbey church call them back to prayer. Some might assume that this is an unhappy group of individuals waiting for some eternal reward. Yet, if you visited St. John's Abbey, you would find monks filled with joy. These men believe that the structures of their daily life lead them to becoming their best selves and to developing life-giving relationships within the community, outside of the community, and most importantly with God. These monks believe that structure provides the order that helps individuals and communities to flourish. Ideally, the church's structures reflect wisdom gained through its tradition and the community's sense of what God is revealing. In this way, structures should be seen as lamps illumining the path of freedom rather than barriers that keep us from it. Therefore, properly understood, structures are among the church's most powerful tools for promoting Christian freedom and well-being.

Practices

Personal conversion and structural reform are crucially important for synodalizing the church, yet they need another dimension as their necessary complement: practices. Here a practice means an action or behavior done regularly or habitually, and often as part of a larger community, which provides a concrete expression of a belief, shaping one's engagement with God and neighbor. Typical examples of practices are the (sub)culture of a given country, group, or family, or the lifestyle of a family of religious life, such as the Benedictines or the Jesuits.

In shaping our behavior, human beings depend very much on something larger than themselves: a culture, a context, a way of proceeding. Modern philosophy and psychology point out that human beings are part of groups. Being related belongs to our very essence and shapes our being and behavior; it also means that our behavior is heavily influenced by others. While attitudes and behavior rest upon one's personal responsibility—the weight of which is underlined with the word *conversion*—relying upon them risks overestimating our capabilities. Hence the importance of practices that help us develop behavior by imitation and osmosis.

Similarly, it is possible to overestimate the power of structural reform. Canon law can prescribe that a bishop has to listen to the faithful, but it cannot force him to have an attitude of respectful and interested listening. Elsewhere I (Jos) have called this one of "the limitations of canonical reform."[19] Structural reform needs to be complemented by what cannot be organized and structured, namely, an authentic mindset and an intrinsic commitment. Earlier we heard Michael Plattig point out that religious communities generally agree that "communal processes need structures, but also attitudes [*Grundhaltungen*]" and that "without the latter a synodal project very quickly fails." That holds true for rules and procedures in general. Yet if our capacity to develop the attitudes and behavior that are needed to cover for the limitations of structural reform is, in fact, limited, we need to look elsewhere. Practices are much more communal. They address what the subjective and personal notion of behavior and the objective notion of structure do not. And so practices, too, are crucial for synodalizing the church.

Thus, synodalizing the church is an exercise of renewal and reform that entails various dimensions, which are treated in more detail in the following chapters: attitudes and behavior (chapter six), structures (chapter seven), and practices (chapter eight).

---

19. Jos Moons, SJ, "La lettre ou l'esprit? La synodalité et les limites de la réforme du droit canon," *Nouvelle Revue Théologique* 145 (2023): 403–19.

From Talking the Talk to Walking the Walk

Synodal Attitudes and Behavior

To grow into a more synodal church, it is crucially important that all of us are involved. Synodality cannot be delegated to our leaders or to a small group of "initiated believers." Because of the incarnating logic of the Christian faith as exemplified by Christ, this involvement of ours needs to be real; we need to "walk the walk" and not just talk. While in official documents for the Synod 2021–24 theologians and pastors often speak in abstract language about inclusion, participation, listening, or collaboration, in this chapter we make a plea for translating those abstract synodal values into concrete attitudes and behavior, and thus to "real-ize" them—make them real. We will highlight four concrete examples of behavior that are required for building a synodal church: listening well, speaking well, waiting and pondering, and journeying together.

The point of this chapter is to explicitly thematize what ecclesiological reflections often leave implicit: the actions that befit a synodal church. There exists a dynamic back-and-forth relationship between theory and practice. Thinking differently about the church will—when these thoughts are integrated into one's whole being—lead to acting differently. But it also works the other way round: by acting differently, we will build up a different faith experience and faith conviction. In more critical terms, if we want to build a synodal church, a unilaterally theoretical discourse misses valuable elements that help to do that.

The importance of concrete behavior was underlined in the previous chapter and it becomes clearer when we consider it in light of baptism. Official documents and theologians have emphasized baptism as the basis of synodality, but they usually focus on baptism as a *state*. The argument runs as follows: as we have all been baptized—clothed with Christ and anointed with the Spirit—all Catholics (and Christians in general) fundamentally share the same dignity and mission. Yet we would like to broaden and dynamize that baptismal foundation of a synodal church by including the notion of *ongoing* conversion. Such an approach is truer to what baptism is: the endpoint of a conversion process that is also an ongoing one that includes living out one's paschal transformation, one's ecclesial incorporation, and one's missionary commitment. Thus, broadening one's notion of baptism from a static "status" to a dynamic calling reflects a fuller and more authentic understanding of the sacrament. It helpfully supports our plea for concrete action towards greater synodality.[1]

It is important to remember that this type of ongoing conversion should avoid a narrowly individualistic focus on "my own" salvation. The International Theological Commission speaks helpfully of a "personal conversion to the spirituality of communion." Such a conversion is a "paschal transition from 'I' understood in a self-centered way to the ecclesial 'we,' where every 'I,' clothed in Christ (cf. Galatians 3:27), lives and jour-

---

1. For elaboration, see Moons, "Broadening the Baptismal Foundation of a Synodal Church."

neys with his or her brothers and sisters as a responsible and active agent of the one mission of the People of God."[2]

Listening Well

So, what helps to walk the synodal walk? In the first place, we should improve the quality of our listening. One important way we can do this is by replacing "Yes, but . . . " responses with "Tell me more!"

In our daily conversation, we often are not really listening but merely waiting to speak. When it is our turn, we start to shed light on different aspects, add valuable nuances, and so on. "Yes, but . . . " comes in handy to turn things around in our direction. Interestingly, the *but* indicates that what we are going to say is different from what our conversation partner has just said. People sometimes get angry at the suggestion that a "Yes, but" response may cut off the other person prematurely and that she may deserve to be listened to a bit more. They object that in a conversation, I can spontaneously present my opinion, experience, or perspective. Surely my thoughts matter as much as those of the person I'm speaking to. Isn't that the point of synodality: that my thoughts matter?

However, the disadvantage of the "Yes, but" style of conversation is that it prevents us from growing more familiar with what our conversation partner thinks, feels, or experiences. Psychology tells us that people need time to disclose their thinking, sentiments, or experience to others (and indeed to themselves). Our own life experience teaches each of us the same thing. Before we share what's really on our mind and on our heart, we want to be sure that the other person is

2. International Theological Commission, Synodality in the Life and Mission of the Church 107, March 2, 2018, https://www.vatican.va/roman _curia/congregations/cfaith/cti_documents/rc_cti_20180302_sinodalita _en.html.

interested. To prevent disappointment, people tend to hide while wanting to be found. The tool of mirroring is helpful for inviting people to disclose themselves: one summarizes what the other person has said and "mirrors" that back to the person.[3] When I respond in this way, I convey the message that I understand what the other person is saying and that I want to know more. Once he feels safe, he takes a next step. Listening well requires great generosity, for the focus is entirely on the other person. Radcliffe expresses this well when he suggests that "we should be gentle midwives to each other's insights, especially when we are uneasy with the ideas that are seeking articulation."[4]

A "Yes, but" response is the exact opposite of such gentle, respectful listening. Responding with "Yes, but" sends the message that there shall be no further exploration of the other person's experiences, sentiments, or thinking; it is time to change the focus of the conversation from the other person to me. In the synodal context, that is ineffective. It leads to superficial knowledge of our fellow pilgrims, so that we are *not* journeying together. It keeps us from discerning together what the Spirit is saying to us now.

Becoming a more synodal person thus requires both unlearning and learning. The learning involves controlling one's spontaneous impulses to speak as well as acquiring facility in another way of responding. Mirroring is certainly helpful, as are various

---

3. Mirroring can be done at various levels, and can be complemented with other types of listening, for example, by exploring images or sentiments. For a practical guide to listening, see Jos Moons, SJ, *The Art of Spiritual Direction: A Guide to Ignatian Practice* (New York: Paulist Press, 2021), or any other practical handbook.

4. Timothy Radcliffe, OP, "Accountability and Co-Responsibility in the Government of the Church: The Example of the Dominicans," *Studia Canonica* 56 (2022): 587–604.

other forms of inviting others to tell more, even the somewhat unpolished "Tell me more." Yet applying tools is not sufficient, as they do not work automatically; the tools must be accompanied by an attitude. Crucial elements of that attitude are, first, a sincere respect for other people and a sincere interest in their story. It can be stretched further to include listening to what is going on in culture, science, politics—or what theologians call the signs of the times. In addition, one needs patience and generosity; these attitudes give space and time, which are crucial for real listening. Finally, listening requires an attitude of wanting to learn rather than wanting to teach.[5]

Speaking Well

To build a more synodal church we not only need people to listen well, but also to *speak* well. Here we encounter a double challenge. The first is to find one's own voice, which requires a certain boldness and which Pope Francis calls *parrhesia*. Recall that Francis stated at the opening of the Synod of the Family (2014), "One general and basic condition is this: speaking honestly. Let no one say: 'I cannot say this, they will think this or this of me . . . '. It is necessary to say with *parrhesia* all that one feels."[6] To describe synodality, both the Preparatory Document and the *Vademecum* quote a comment that Francis made at the opening of the 2018 Synod on Young People, the Faith, and Vocational Discernment: "The Synod we are living is a moment of sharing. I wish, therefore, at the

---

5. For a deeper grounding of listening and of the attitudes it supposes, see what Randall Rosenberg says about "authentic docility" as a "foundational virtue," in Rosenberg, "Cultivating a Synodal Disposition in Theological Education," 335–36.

6. Pope Francis, Greeting of Pope Francis to the Synod Fathers during the First General Congregation.

beginning of the Synod Assembly, to invite everyone to speak with courage and frankness (*parrhesia*), namely to integrate freedom, truth and charity. Only dialogue can help us grow. An honest, transparent critique is constructive and helpful, and does not engage in useless chatter, rumors, conjectures or prejudices."[7]

Speaking up always means taking a risk: one does not know how it will be received. Humanly speaking, we do not always have such courage. It is tempting to keep up appearances and to either "say the right things" or keep our mouth shut. (In those cases, we usually do, in fact, speak, but rather behind closed doors in the form of complaining, gossiping, or speaking our mind in the safe bubble of friends.) Let us also admit that ecclesial culture has not exactly promoted *parrhesia*.

Thus, the challenge of *parrhesia* requires psychological and spiritual growth. We need a mature self-confidence so that we "own" our perspective and articulate it, even if it is not liked or fashionable. (That maturity should also allow us to hear other views openly.) Deep roots of faith in God as our ultimate guide and judge will spiritually equip and strengthen us to speak up without self-censoring.[8]

The second challenge is to use our voice calmly, clearly, and to the point. If people feel that they have not been listened to, they tend to speak *loudly* and with lots of emotion; public manifestations with banners, whistles, and sometimes riots are examples of that type of speaking. While speaking loudly certainly draws attention, the result is that one needs to do

---

7. Pope Francis, Greeting to the Synod Fathers; and Pope Francis, Address at the Opening of the Synod of Bishops on Young People, the Faith, and Vocational Discernment. Cf. General Secretariat for the Synod, *Vademecum* 2.3: "Being synodal requires time for sharing: We are invited to speak with authentic courage and honesty (*parrhesia*) in order to integrate freedom, truth, and charity. Everyone can grow in understanding through dialogue." See also *Vademecum* 5.3 and Preparatory Document 30.

8. See Plattig, "Gehorsam: Grundhaltung für synodale Prozesse," 101–2.

considerable sifting before we reach the stage of discerning what the Spirit is saying to the churches in that. Speaking calmly, clearly, and to the point is much more useful—and much more difficult. It requires preparation and discipline. Instead of going with the flow of one's emotions and thoughts, one first seeks inner clarification and purification: What is going on within me? Which sentiments are helpful and which ones are not? Shall I accuse, judge, seek revenge? Or shall I seek the greater glory of God and the growth of the kingdom, in a humble and confident authenticity that takes into account myself as well as others? Which thoughts are digressions and should better be left out? Can I structure my thoughts and sentiments so that those who listen to me can actually follow? Have the words I want to speak been purified by silence?

Certain concrete rules can help. These include:

- preparing one's contribution by writing it down

- distinguishing clear points in one's speaking (and keeping their number limited)

- speaking from "I" instead of from "you" or "they"

- distinguishing facts, feelings, proposals, and so on

- not speaking too long

Here we could draw on resources such as nonviolent communication. This communication method seeks to structure the confusing and explosive mix of emotions, thoughts, and judgements in such a way that we can have meaningful, open conversations about difficult topics without ending up in a fight. It typically structures communication in four elements: observing what has happened, naming how that makes one feel, articulating what one needs, and formulating a request.[9]

---

9. See the classic Marshall B. Rosenberg, *Non-Violent Communication: A Language of Life*, 3rd ed. (Encinitas, CA: PuddleDancer, 2019). For its

Both listening well and speaking well require training. Here established practices such as conversation in the Spirit—presented in chapter three—can help us to build up a training routine. As it imposes certain ways of responding and forbids others, it helps us to get used to a new way of proceeding. For example, by not allowing participants to respond directly, conversation in the Spirit trains us to make space for others instead of being dominated by our own dearly cherished thoughts. We are invited to contemplate what God is saying through the words of others and to seek truth beyond ourselves. Ideally those new attitudes become a habit, so that we can also use them outside of the strict straitjacket of more formal occasions of conversation in the Spirit. It certainly helps when training sessions lead to a positive experience. Here it is worthwhile to recall how participants of the synodal sessions, both locally and in Rome, have often spoken very positively of what they have lived. It is new, but good.

Waiting and Pondering

In the third place, to build a more synodal church we need to learn to wait and ponder. Listening well and speaking well bring to the surface a host of feelings, thoughts, views, and proposals. The point of welcoming those is to discern what the Holy Spirit is saying to the church. In other words, once the material is on the table, we should take the time to sit with ourselves and with God and weigh—or ponder—what was said.

This is a deeply personal affair. Pondering requires an engagement with one's interiority and cannot be replaced with consulting Scripture, the Catechism, or another authority or

---

application to synodality, see Mary Lilian Akhere Ehidiamhen, "A Synodal Alternative for Ecclesial Conflict: Marshall Rosenberg's Nonviolent Communication," *Journal of Moral Theology* 11/2 (2022): 45–64.

source. Here an old desert father adage holds true: "Go, sit in your cell, and your cell will teach you everything."[10] This was reportedly how Abba Moses, a figure of authority whose counsel was often sought, answered a younger monk who wanted "a word" from him. Abba Moses's advice was to seek wisdom by sitting with himself, in the silence and seclusion of his monastic cell, instead of relying on others.

As the desert fathers then and contemplative monks and sisters now know, spending time with oneself in silence is not easy. One becomes aware of one's superficial desires, spontaneous yet unhelpful inclinations, prejudices, judgements, past experiences, psychological or spiritual patterns, and so on. Acknowledging the extent to which one is marked by those desires, judgements, memories, and more is deeply humbling. Yet for that very same reason, it is crucial for the type of pondering that we need in a synodal church. It relativizes our spontaneous assessments, as those may be marked by our troubled interiority rather than the Holy Spirit, and thereby it opens us to new perspectives.[11]

In addition to spending time with oneself and thus, as it were, pondering oneself, one needs to ponder content: the various possible thoughts, feelings, options, views that are on

---

10. Benedicta Ward, SLG, ed. and trans., *The Sayings of the Desert Fathers* (Kalamazoo, MI: Cistercian Publications, 1975), 139. Note that there were also desert mothers (or ammas).

11. Plattig elaborates introspection as part of his exploration of obedience in Plattig, "Gehorsam: Grundhaltung für synodale Prozesse," 90–92. Cf. what Robert Doran called psychic conversion, as summarized by Randall Rosenberg: "The experience of trauma, painful memories, and a wounded imagination requires psychic conversion. . . . Psychic conversion attends to the way these narratives, images, and symbols impact our affective dispositions and spontaneous responses. It involves the transformation of the imagination from repressive, damaging symbols to healing, redemptive symbols." Rosenberg, "Cultivating a Synodal Disposition in Theological Education," 340–42.

the table. This is typically done in an in-between space. We have not arrived at clarity yet, so we need to wait and be open to what Pope Francis likes to call the surprises of the Spirit. Or, in more challenging terms, whoever sets out on a quest for the Spirit needs to bear unclarity and uncertainty. Unfortunately for those of us who may be uncomfortable with such experiences, both on the traditionalist and liberal side of the spectrum, that means that a certain amount of confusion is unavoidable—one may even go so far as saying that it is *essential* for any process of discernment. The way forward is to pray for the grace of letting go of everything except God, which Ignatian language calls "interior freedom."

How do we navigate the confusion that unavoidably marks our waiting-and-pondering adventure? The Ignatian tradition offers two considerations that help to calibrate our compass.

First is the experience of *consolation* or *desolation*. When a given thought, feeling, idea, or project comes with a sense of faith, hope, joy, love, mercy, or clarity, Ignatius calls this consolation. By means of these interior sentiments, God encourages us, as if he is saying, "Go on. This is the right path." It is important to note, though, that consolation is not the same as "what feels great," for experiences like mercy are often quite subtle. Trappist sister Rebekka Willekes, prioress of the priory of Klaarland in Belgium, testifies that "when there is a sense of peace, communion, and joy, these are strong indications that a decision does come from the Spirit."[12] On the other hand, we may experience a sort of aftertaste that is rather bitter, dark, confused, complex, or hopeless. This Ignatius calls *desolation*. Overriding sentiments of distrust and fear suggest that it is not God who is inspiring us but something else. In other words, paying attention to the interior "aftertaste" is one way to allow God to guide us. The presup-

---

12. Rebekka Willekes, OCSO, "Synodal Wisdom from the Rule of Benedict," in *Witnesses of Synodality*, ed. Moons, 11.

position is that God will confirm and encourage us on the good path with an enduring consolation.

A second criterion seeks the exterior fruits. If we go with a given thought, feeling, idea, or project, what happens? Does it build up the kingdom or not? Does it promote salvation and well-being or not? Does it increase faith, hope, joy, love, and mercy? Once again, the presupposition is that God will confirm and encourage us on the good path through the good fruits that emerge.

Importantly, waiting and pondering is a slow affair. It takes time for us to grow in humility and to unmask un-Godly considerations. Deception looms large. The bad spirit may suggest seemingly pious considerations that are not, in fact, of God. Therefore, Ignatius recommends being very attentive to how views or plans or sentiments unfold: What comes out of them? We need to take the long view.[13] Another crucial piece of advice is to seek God in subtlety rather than overriding clarity. God's voice (or whatever image one may prefer) is often very modest. Ignatius uses the telling image of water falling on a sponge or on a rock. God's voice is gentle: "The good angel touches the soul sweetly, lightly and gently, like a drop of water going into a sponge." By contrast, the bad spirit's voice is loud and clear, "as when a drop of water falls on a stone."[14]

Here, too, unlearning and learning go hand in hand. We need to learn to wait and to grow a habit of "sitting in our cell." A second thing we need to learn is to befriend our interiority and to learn our way around it. This includes humbly acknowledging all that is going on inside, over against our tendency to think, act, discuss. It also comes with greater familiarity with

13. Cf. Rules of Discernment, second series, rules 4–6, in Ignatius of Loyola, *Spiritual Exercises* 332–34 (*Saint Ignatius of Loyola: Personal Writings*, trans. Joseph A. Muñitiz and Philip Endean [London: Penguin, 1996]).

14. Rules of Discernment, second series, rule 7, in Ignatius of Loyola, *Spiritual Exercises* 335.

a new set of criteria for truth-finding. The church needs "an affective reconfiguration," that is, a more positive appreciation of the affective and spiritual wisdom of the discernment of spirits, of our interior movements and thoughts.[15]

In regard to learning to wait and to ponder, the practice adopted in the synod sessions of keeping silence after each intervention can certainly serve as an inspiration. Practices such as a daily "review" of the day and what it has brought—what the Ignatian tradition calls the Examen Prayer—can be beneficial in helping us develop a practice of pondering.[16]

Ultimately, the goal is to make waiting and pondering part of our standard practice of Christian living; they should be considered as important as reading the gospels, participating in the Eucharist, and serving one's neighbor.

Journeying *Together*

So far, we have focused on what individual persons can do. With their listening, speaking, and pondering, they can contribute to building a more synodal church. A crucial element that needs to be added is that these efforts should be part of a larger project of journeying together.

For example, journeying together is essential for discernment, for one cannot do discernment on one's own. While we said earlier that seeking God is a personal affair, it is not an *individual* affair. Discernment needs the help of other people; we should converse about what we experience. Others may identify blind spots or may confirm our discernment. If "I" am the only person with a certain sentiment, view, or perspective, that is usually a bad sign. Thus, we need to learn to share about our discernment and get others involved.

---

15. Cf. Jos Moons, SJ, "Synodality and Discernment: The Affective Reconfiguration of the Church," *Studia Canonica* 56 (2022): 379–93.

16. See Mark Thibodeaux, SJ, *Reimagining the Ignatian Examen: Fresh Ways to Pray from Your Day* (Chicago: Loyola Press, 2015).

That holds all the more true for synodality, as it is commonly understood as *common* discernment. The point is not that *I* discern but that *we* discern. Beyond a readiness to bear other views—which is already a challenge—we seek what truth, wisdom, desires, and needs are being communicated in our conversation. Stefan Mangnus's comment concerning the Dominican tradition's love for debates, as exemplified in Thomas Aquinas's style of doing theology, sheds light on common discernment also: "The purpose of a debate is not to defeat the other but to come closer to a shared truth."[17] Therefore, the focus should not be on myself but on what is going on around me. Another source of insight here is the chapter in the Benedictine tradition, that is, a regular meeting of the monks of a monastery to discuss the business of the community. Rebekka Willekes helpfully explains that the point of participation in the chapter is not what I say but what I hear and what God thus reveals.[18]

Common discernment rarely leads to unanimity. If that is so, how to journey together? First, it is crucially important that we grow in a sense of brother- and sisterhood. While holding different views, we share the journey; we are fellow pilgrims. Living that brother- and sisterhood goes beyond discernment or decision-making; here journeying together is understood in a very broad sense.

For example, speaking about Dominican spirituality, Radcliffe underlines the importance of friendship. The communitarian form of government and the chapters, as the concrete expressions thereof, should be understood and lived in a context of brother- and sisterhood flowing over into friendship: "Decision

17. Stefan Mangnus, OP, "Dominican Gifts for a Synodal Church," in *Witnesses of Synodality*, ed. Moons, 24–25.

18. Willekes, "Synodal Wisdom from the Rule of Benedict," 8: "The type of meeting Benedict intends, however, is not what I may want to say, but what I may hear. Or rather, what the Lord wants me to hear and, thereby, to reveal to me."

making takes place within the context of hours of praying together, listening to each other preach and share our faith, eating and recreating together."[19] As we will see in chapter eight, Benedictine authors underline the value of the shared life in a monastery. Both take away the focus from deliberations and content, and propose a much broader horizon of brotherhood, sisterhood, and friendship. We need to spend time together, pray together, laugh together, and so on. Speaking and listening make more sense if they are part of a general culture of journeying together.

In the second place, we should embrace diversity. Instead of an artificial view of unity as uniformity, we should acknowledge the reality: Catholics hold different views and appreciate different practices. (The diversity of religious orders speaks volumes.) Obviously, that diversity is rooted in some shared convictions. All Christians confess God as Father, Son, and Spirit, yet the way we interpret the Trinity and, for example, God's fatherhood differs. To bear diversity, it may help to recall that the word *catholic* meant originally "universal" or "all-encompassing." It may also help to acknowledge that seeking the truth usually involves debate. Therefore, we should have a positive view of disagreements.[20] What we need for that in terms of attitudes is a great generosity towards views that are not one's own, as well as creativity and a willingness to compromise. Those whose view is not followed should have been heard and listened to. Ideally, they should also *feel* heard.

In the third place, we should accept that at some stage a decision is taken—either by the majority or by the leader—and we should accept that decision, even if it differs from what we ourselves had imagined. That is not to say that such decisions cannot be reconsidered. For example, a lack of real re-

---

19. Radcliffe, "Accountability and Co-Responsibility," 598.

20. See Judith Gruber, "Consensus or Dissensus? Exploring the Theological Role of Conflict in a Synodal Church," *Louvain Studies* 43 (2020): 239–59.

ception suggests that the decision is not generally felt to be wise and that a new process of discernment is needed. In any case, greater transparency on the procedures to reach decisions and on the reasons for a given decision will be very helpful. We should therefore rejoice that transparency and its sister notion, accountability, have become more and more important in synodal documents. For example, speaking about deacons and priests, the Synthesis Report 2023 stated that "transparency and a culture of accountability are of crucial importance for us to move forward in building a synodal church."[21]

Conclusion

The future of synodality depends greatly on how we *behave*. Greater insight into synodality and structural reform are not sufficient; we need to live synodality in our actions. Synodality ultimately requires specific behavior. As we have argued in chapter five, that behavior is both rooted in faith convictions and builds up faith convictions: *lex vivendi lex credendi*. Four aspects of that behavior were highlighted: listening well, speaking well, waiting and pondering, and journeying together. They lead to types of conversation that are distinct from arguments, discussions, or debates, and that are ultimately contemplative.

As the faithful and our leaders have received little or no training in those areas and in that type of conversation, we suggest that developing training in this regard is of the highest importance. It recalls the topic of formation that has become a major issue in official documents and synodal literature, and that was treated in chapter four. Importantly, though, that should be practical—and not just theological—training.[22]

---

21. Synthesis Report 2023, 11k. Although not explicitly stated, the same holds true for bishops.

22. Helpfully, the International Theological Commission spoke in its 2018 document, Synodality in the Life and Mission of the Church, of the importance of "disciplined training for welcoming and listening to one another,"

Importantly, too, the training of the leaders has priority, as they can set the tone. Speaking about the bishop, the Synthesis Report 2023 promoted teaching by example and explained rightly that "the conviction with which the bishop himself adopts a synodal approach and the style by which he exercises authority will influence decisively how priests and deacons, lay men and women, and those in consecrated life, participate in the synodal process."[23] Practically speaking, as we saw in chapter four, focusing on seminaries, novitiate, and post-novitiate training may be a good idea.

Finally, we should not underestimate the role that each and every one can play. We do not need permission to start listening better, speaking out humbly yet confidently, pondering attentively all that we hear, and journeying together while bearing diversity. Here the term *informal synodality* is really helpful. Synodality exists not only in the form of formalized processes with invitation from the Vatican; we build up a synodal church whenever we share our faith, pray together, seek greater insight, and listen to what the Spirit is saying to the churches. In short, all of us can contribute to building up a synodal church; the future of synodality depends greatly on how *we* behave.[24]

---

alongside "conversion of heart and mind," adding that "without [those] the external instruments of communion would be of hardly any use" (107).

23. Synthesis Report 2023, 12c.

24. See the Preparatory Document 27, elaborated in Alphonse Borras, "Ecclesial Synodality, Participatory Processes, and Decision-Making Procedures: A Canonist's Point of View," in *For a Missionary Reform of the Church: The* Civiltà Cattolica *Seminar*, ed. Antonio Spadaro, SJ, and Carlos M. Galli, 218–48 (Mahwah, NJ: Paulist Press, 2017).

Chapter Seven

Synodalizing Structures

Local, Regional, and Universal

A key aspect of achieving a synodalization of the entire church is the development of increasingly synodal structures. The theological commitments described in the previous chapters, commitments that reflect some of the deepest aspects of the church's identity, cannot remain theoretical. They must shape the church's structures, including its offices, modes of governance, and laws/rules at the local, regional, and universal levels. In fact, these theological commitments give these structures their intelligibility and meaning. While people often dismiss ecclesial structures as merely bureaucratic or administrative, they provide some of the most concrete ways that the People of God experience the church, for better or worse. They therefore have the potential to offer a direct experience of synodality and come to know its meaning. With that in mind, we can ask: What structures best promote the church's ability to listen and walk together? How can the church update its structures in ways that honor the witness of tradition and meet the needs of today? Becoming a wholly synodal church requires a transformation of ecclesial structures at every level—local, regional, and universal—so that they reflect our beliefs and enable the People of God to walk together.

The Local Level

Synodal ecclesiology finds its starting point at the local level. Rather than looking at Rome first, synodality says, "Let's start with where we are: my parish, my diocese, my community." This starting point reflects the ancient teaching that the church exists in and from the local churches (*in quibus et ex quibus*). The language of "local church" can convey a variety of entities, including a parish, a grouping of parishes, or a diocese. It can also connote gatherings that transect parishes or dioceses, including apostolic movements or lay religious societies. How can the decisions at this level be reached in a more inclusive way and thus better reflect the experience of the faithful?

This chapter will treat four ideas vital to a synodalization of local structures and decision-making. The first concerns an approach to decision-making marked by broad and dynamic participation. The second involves formation to prepare the faithful to engage in communal discernment. The third is the imperative that experiences of Christ and community necessarily provide the backdrop for creating and sustaining synodal decision-making practices. And finally, the fourth relates to the development of pastoral councils at the parish and diocesan levels that serve as centers for participatory governance. When topics like these are engaged in an effort to realize the vibrancy and centrality of local ecclesial structures, there is an opportunity to reduce the distance between people's everyday experience of the church's life and structures that express it.

There is an impression in the church today that only those individuals entrusted with taking a final decision have power. This contributes to a sense that only a small minority of the faithful are empowered to utilize the gifts given to them by the Holy Spirit. Therefore, an initial question is: How do we reimagine decision-taking in such a way that everybody can contribute? Synod documents have argued that a first step lies in making a distinction between decision-making and decision-taking.[1] Decision-making connotes a complex process involving several stages, only one of which is making a final choice. In this process, responsibility is shared among decision-makers even though not all are responsible for "taking" the final choice. Decision-makers include creative people who generate ideas, people who contribute diverse perspectives, and those who offer historical experiences. They also include people who gather the necessary facts, groups who implement decisions, and those who can evaluate the outcomes. This process also requires a decision-taker, an individual or a group charged with accounting for all that has been presented and then, on behalf of the entire community, reaching a final choice. A key role of the decision-taker is to help facilitate the process by calling out the gifts of all the community members and bringing them together as a whole. A synodal church necessarily sees decision-making as a process characterized by differentiated participation. Decision-making and decision-taking are two moments within one process; these moments are not to be seen as separate or competitive but as mutually reenforcing.

Here we can draw on an example provided by an esteemed twentieth-century professor of canon law, Robert T. Kennedy, who wrote a highly regarded article on shared responsibility in decision-making. He invokes a parable used in Plato's *Republic*. The story speaks of a ship captain and his crew. Each of the

---

1. For more on the distinction between decision-making and decision-taking see the International Theological Commission's document Synodality in the Life and Mission of the Church 69. Luciani discusses the significance of this distinction in *Synodality: A New Way of Proceeding in the Church*, 39–42.

sailors is eager to take the wheel from the captain, yet none of them actually knows how to navigate the vessel. Plato notes that these people "have no idea that the true navigator must study the seasons of the year, the sky, the stars, the winds and other professional subjects, if he is to be really fit to control a ship."[2] Once members of the crew prevail and take over the helm, they do not know how to reach their destination; they fail to realize that sailing involves more than just the ability to steer the wheel. Kennedy likens this account to the way that governance in the church encompasses more than the right to cast a vote or make a final choice. He notes, "To hold the helm of a ship without knowledge of the sea, the winds, the tides, the stars, and one's own ship is to imperil the lives of everyone on board. So, to participate in ecclesial governance without acquired knowledge not only of ecclesiology but also of governance and its manifold processes, is to imperil the ecclesial life of the community in which one governs."[3]

A second piece of creating synodal structures on the local level involves forming people with an awareness that the Holy Spirit directs and inspires authentic ecclesial decision-making. Participants must come to the process with an understanding that the purpose is not to determine the will of the majority or to have one's own views reflected in the outcome; instead, synodality asks the community to discern collectively how the Holy Spirit is speaking to the church in this moment. This method of decision-making reflects not only the baptismal dignity of all the People of God, but it also reflects the way that God's revelation is communal. All the People of God must receive formation that helps them engage in prayerful listening and open themselves to growth in understanding. Developing a culture of shared responsibility in communal

---

2. Robert T. Kennedy, "Shared Responsibility in Ecclesial Decision-Making," *Studia Canonica* 14 (1980): 5.

3. Kennedy, "Shared Responsibility in Ecclesial Decision-Making," 6.

decision-making requires a climate in which there is willingness to mutually seek God's will in humility and openness to the guidance of the Holy Spirit, a climate where there is an acceptance of the fact that responsibility is shared even though not all are "decision-takers."

Thirdly, developing synodal structures on the local level requires that communities focus not only on participatory decision-making and on formation in discerning together, but also promoting authentic experiences of Christ. Communal discernment and differentiated decision-making require patience, trust, and commitment. Such processes inevitably include delays and potential disappointment. To endure these challenges and hold the community together amidst them, people must experience the church as a place where they encounter Christ and feel their gifts are called forth and actualized. It is experience, ultimately, that animates and sustains people on the synodal journey. Experiences of Christ as the one who consoles us, serves us, opens up new horizons, and reveals to us our true identity provide the essential context for making ecclesial decision-making viable and meaningful. Such experiences enable people to endure taxing ecclesial processes with patience and trust. Experiences allow believers to know that while the roles in decision-making are different, a shared purpose guides the outcome with the Holy Spirit directing the end. Many people today lack patience to wait for the church to provide satisfying answers to their questions or speak to matters that they care about, precisely because they have not experienced or recognized life-giving encounters with Christ in the church that give them confidence to stay and undertake their co-responsibility. Therefore, efforts to create synodal structures on the local level must direct energy to cultivating the types of experiences that provide the necessary context for ecclesial decision-making. A synodal church realizes that one of the most important parts of helping the faithful walk together is providing experiences along the way that unite, enliven, and bond us as a community.

Finally, synodalizing the church's local level requires developing a dynamic role for pastoral councils as generative bodies that enact shared responsibility and participative governance. Pastoral council gatherings are meetings where the faithful speak directly to their priest or bishop, revealing their needs, possible solutions to existing problems, and the feasibility of plans and proposals presented to the community.[4] Parish and diocesan pastoral councils offer natural spaces for spiritual conversation and mutual listening. Unsurprisingly, therefore, various official documents on synodality recommend the pastoral councils as "indispensable" instruments within a synodal church.[5] These councils exist in many dioceses and parishes as a vibrant structure for lay participation, offering vital points of convergence for discerning the *sensus fidelium*. In them, ordained leaders, including bishops and priests, can both listen and teach; likewise, the laity may use the space both for formation and expression of the *sensus fidelium*.

To promote the functioning of these councils, they need to become more common and active. In addition, they must organize themselves as something other than legislative bodies that work through pre-set agendas and vote on policy outcomes. Rather, they must regularize a local space where spiritual conversation and discernment take place, and which actively invites people—far beyond the council members themselves—to share what the Holy Spirit is revealing to them. These types of interactions can be moments of formation that allow all the faithful—laity and ordained alike—to grow. Synodalizing the church requires more effective pastoral councils where the entire People of God—the laity, together with their

---

4. See Wijlens, "Reforming the Church by Hitting the Reset Button," 260.

5. Document for the Continental Stage 78; cf. *Instrumentum Laboris* 2023, B 3.3, and Synthesis Report 2023, 12k.

priests and bishops—explores how to deal with particular challenges and opportunities and advance the church's mission of spreading the Gospel.

The Regional Level

The Catholic Church has clear and decisive structures of authority and governance on the universal level (Rome) and on the local level (dioceses), but it has less clear and decisive structures at the regional level, that is, at the national or continental levels. If these structures are in place—for example, national bishops' conferences like the USCCB or continental conferences like the Latin American and Caribbean Episcopal Council, better known as CELAM—their authority is often unclear. We propose that a synodal church should also look to regional structures as an aspect of its organization, because they possess immense potential to promote the aims of synodality and perceive the *sensus fidei*.

Some have cautioned against developing such bodies, arguing that they are not inherent to the church's nature in the same way as the universal and local levels. Instead, some critics see regional structures as human constructions and historically contingent. Others have advised caution about developing national or regional centers of authority out of a fear that they may come to be viewed as points of unity that could serve as alternatives to Rome. These concerns need to be considered in any movement towards developing or expanding regional models of authority. In an increasingly global and synodal church, however, such instruments possess great potential for enhancing the catholicity of the church's listening and its ability to make decisions closer to their point of origin or impact.

Pope Francis advocated for developing and empowering regional bodies in the church from the beginning of his pontificate. Among the many firsts that mark Francis's papacy, he is the first pope who previously served as the president of an episcopal conference. As the Archbishop of Buenos Aires, he spent six years (2005–2011) as the president of the Argentine Episcopal Conference. In this role, he developed an appreciation for the way that regional authorities can work as positive and powerful centripetal forces that serve both the universal church and the local churches. This insight is clearly expressed in *Evangelii Gaudium*, which speaks forcefully about the need for ecclesial decentralization: "Excessive centralization, rather than proving helpful, complicates the Church's life and her missionary outreach" (EG 32). Francis calls the church to a greater appreciation of local and regional elements and notes that central bureaucracy is not sufficient; there is also a need for increased collegiality and solidarity. What is needed is not unanimity but true unity in the richness of diversity. In a climactic passage, *Evangelii Gaudium* assert the pope's belief that "the papal magisterium should not be expected to offer a definitive or complete word on every question which effects the church and the world. It is not advisable for the pope to take the place of local bishops in the discernment of every issue which arises in their territory. In this sense, I am conscious of the need to promote a sound 'decentralization'" (EG 16).

A "sound decentralization" in a synodal church requires expanding ways that episcopal conferences might make authoritative decisions for their regions. The effort to create a more synodal church includes efforts to empower episcopal conferences to listen more effectively and act on what they hear. Further, it might involve allowing episcopal conferences, in certain circumstances, to submit ideas for synodal agendas, appeal decisions of the Holy See, and consult on aspects of doctrinal decision-making.[6] The importance of regional ecclesial bodies is also affirmed in Francis's practice of punctuating

---

6. See Hervé Legrand, OP, "*Communio Ecclesiae, Communio Ecclesiarum, Collegium Episcoporum,*" in *For a Missionary Reform of the Church*, ed. Spadaro and Galli, 184.

his writings with references to documents authored by regional episcopal bodies, including the Latin American Episcopal Council (CELAM), the Federation of Asian Bishops' Conferences (FABC), and the Symposium of Episcopal Conferences of Africa (SECAM). We also see it in the way that national, regional, and continental bodies played a prominent role throughout the synod process.

A "sound decentralization" in a synodal church requires regional gatherings beyond episcopal conferences that allow for broader and more diverse participation. Here, the First Ecclesial Assembly of Latin America and the Caribbean (2021) serves as a model. The bishops of CELAM have gathered for five episcopal conferences over the course of fifty-two years. These meetings were held in Rio de Janeiro, Brazil (1955), Medellín, Columbia (1968), Puebla, Mexico (1979), Santo Domingo, Dominican Republic (1992), and Aparecida, Brazil (2007). Widely considered to be effective examples of regional ecclesial collaboration, the five CELAM conferences have helped these churches to navigate critical opportunities and challenges facing the larger region. Birgit Weiler notes that these gatherings "were characterized by close attention to the signs of the times, a careful and collective discernment of these signs in light of the gospel, and an interest in discovering God's will for the life and mission of the church in the current context."[7] As Weiler also notes, Pope Francis suggested in 2019 that going forward, the region's bishops should take a more participatory approach by holding an ecclesial assembly, allowing for more lay participants, instead of a sixth CELAM conference, which would largely be comprised of bishops. Francis thus indicated a preference for regional gatherings that invite the participation of all the faithful. His hopes were brought to fruition in January 2021, with the First Ecclesial

---

7. Weiler, "Synodality in a Continental Perspective," 133.

Assembly of Latin America and the Caribbean. Addressing the participants by video, Francis shared his hope for the gathering: "May this Assembly not be an elite group separated from the holy, faithful people of God." He continued, "Together with the people. Do not forget it. We are all part of the people of God."[8] Ultimately, regional bodies can provide a unique space for synodal listening where the catholicity of the church can come to life; for this to be realized, their theological status should be taken seriously, and their membership should include lay people.

The advent of continental assemblies in February and March of 2023 is one of the most important and least discussed developments that arose from the Synod on Synodality. In the over-two-thousand-year history of the church, there has never been a time when continental assemblies across the globe gathered simultaneously to discern regional questions and matters of importance to the universal church. For this reason, in terms of ecclesial structures, the synod can be described as a "disruptor," in the sense that the business, tech, and pop culture sectors have recently used the term. A disruptor is something that causes things to change rapidly and in previously unimaginable ways.[9]

Further, the creation of continental assemblies yielded more than one model for this type of instrument; it provided seven. Each of the seven continental assemblies manifested distinct

8. Courtney Mares, "Pope Francis Tells Latin American Ecclesial Assembly Not to Be Elitist," Catholic News Agency, January 25, 2021, https://www.catholicnewsagency.com/news/246229/pope-francis-tells-latin-american-ecclesial-assembly-not-to-be-elitist.

9. We may comparably call COVID-19 a disruptor, because the pandemic and the circumstances it created prompted the astoundingly quick development of nascent technologies and structures, such as the use of Zoom, models of hybrid learning, and food delivery, which on their own might have taken years to develop. In a similar way, the synod accelerated the development of structures for regional discernment.

approaches to how this type of consultation might happen in terms of who should participate, how the process of discernment might unfold, the role of prayer and liturgy, and more.[10] They also challenged the church to think about the relationship of its unity and its diversity, both in terms of what the local and regional churches offer to the church universal and how doctrines can be explained, applied, and adapted in such a way that they can bear fruit in every context.[11]

Within the Synod on Synodality itself, too, new forms of regional structures emerged that may model future ones. For example, as we have seen, the synod required a stage of discernment on the continental level with a twofold purpose: first, a *restitutio* where the regional churches considered whether what was said in the local phase was heard correctly, and second, a chance for regional conversations and reflection on what the consultation at the local phase revealed. To prepare for these gatherings, in late 2022, the Secretariat for the Synod asked the episcopal conferences for their sense of whether the membership of these assemblies should consist only of bishops (an episcopal assembly) or if it should also include wider membership from the People of God (an ecclesial assembly). The responses conveyed a strong desire that representatives from the entire People of God be involved in the continental stage. Thus, the Synod on Synodality did not convene as a traditional gathering of the Synod of Bishops. Rather, it called together representatives from the whole People of God in new ways.

Finally, it merits highlighting that synodality not only values new instruments for listening on the regional level but also links the various levels to one another; the result is a back-and-forth process between the local, regional, and universal

---

10. For an excellent survey of the continental assemblies in 2023, see Wijlens and Tirimanna, *People of God Have Spoken.*

11. Wijlens and Tirimanna, "Introduction," 14.

levels. This is clear in the remarkable way that the Synod on Synodality unfolded. In 2021, Pope Francis called for a synod at the universal level, yet he mandated that it should start with listening in every diocese: the local level should provide input for the universal-level gathering. After listening sessions in parishes and dioceses, the results were gathered at the level of national episcopal conferences, which, as we have seen, is one of the regional levels. The episcopal conferences reflected on these reports and sent their syntheses to Rome (universal level). Rome, then, developed a synthesis of these national reports and sent that document to the churches at the continental level for reflection (another regional level). These reports became the basis for the synod's first *Instrumentum Laboris*, which was the focus for the discussions at the Extraordinary Meeting of the Bishops in Rome in 2023 (universal level). That gathering generated questions which were sent back to the national churches (regional level) to be discussed in the dioceses and parishes (local level). Reports from this second round of local consultation were sent to national episcopal conferences (regional level) and then to Rome (universal level) to inform the second *Instrumentum Laboris* for the final gathering of the synod in October of 2024 (universal level). While this description can seem like a logistical litany, it nevertheless describes a new, synodal way of being church where local, regional, and universal ecclesial structures work together to listen and respond to the People of God.

The Universal Level

Finally, we turn to considering synodal structures at the church's universal level. There are a variety of instruments at this level, including the papacy, the synod of bishops, the Curia, and canon law. In light of the urgent questions regarding the role of the pope in a church seeking a "sound decentralization," we will focus here on the nature of the papacy in a synodal church. How can Rome continue to promote a strong sense of ecclesial unity while also ensuring the inclusion of diverse voices in governance and decision-making processes, so that synodality is also lived out at the universal level?

Rome plays an indispensable role in the Catholic Church as a point of unity and a force for preserving the church's identity. Yet concentrating too much authority in Rome can have a freezing effect whereby the church becomes immobile, like ice, and insufficiently responsive to the needs of local communities. A key element of becoming a listening church involves recognizing that the center ought not to do all the talking; rather it exists, in large part, to facilitate conversations that promote diverse voices. This type of service underscores that a synodal church takes the form of an "inverted pyramid" where the "top is located beneath the base."[12] In such a church, "those who exercise authority are called 'ministers,' because, in the original meaning of the word, they are the least of all."[13] Thus, in a synodal church that adopts the shape of an inverted pyramid, leadership is understood as service and, in particular, the pope is the "servant of the servants of God." The papacy plays an important role in a synodal, inverted church; both have the potential to serve as powerful catalysts for synodal transformation.

Exploring the essence of the papal office helps to elucidate and determine its vital role in a synodal church. If we look at the origins of the papacy, one of its key functions is to safeguard the church's unity. This can be seen in the title *pontiff*, which comes from the Latin word for bridge (*pons*, from which come the Italian, French, and Spanish words for bridge: *ponte*, *pont*, and *puente*, respectively) and the verb for doing or making (*facere*). The pope is a bridge-builder who holds

12. Pope Francis, Ceremony Commemorating 50th Anniversary.
13. Pope Francis, Ceremony Commemorating 50th Anniversary.

the whole church together in right belief (orthodoxy) and right practice (orthopraxis).

This notion of conserving unity is often misconstrued as rooted in an exercise of juridical power. However, papal authority does not first and foremost concern the brute exercise of power; it instead reflects a special relationship between God and the church. Christians have held, going all the way back to the New Testament, that Christ's promise to remain in the church means that the church enjoys the guidance of the Holy Spirit, who leads it to all truth (see Jn 16:13). This is known as the doctrine of ecclesial indefectibility. The belief that God guides the church and preserves it, as a totality, from error includes a belief that God provides instruments that allow the church to know this guidance and express its identity in ways that the community recognizes as authentic. For Catholics, the office of the papacy is one of these instruments. Therefore, the papacy should not be understood as a purely human construction; it is a divine gift that maintains the church in fidelity to the Gospel. Obedience to the pope follows as an expression of confidence in Christ's promises and the Holy Spirit's ongoing direction of the People of God to all truth. Therefore, properly understood, the papacy is not about power, but about a close relationship between God and his church. Papal authority exists as a gift given to the whole church—a corollary of the promise of divine guidance and a means of enabling the successor of Peter to "keep watch" (*episkopein*) over the health and unity of its body.

The manner in which the papacy works to preserve the church's unity naturally looks different at different times in history. The axiom *Ecclesia semper reformanda* and the theological horizon advanced by Vatican II call for ongoing development of the structural expressions of papal authority. The synodal church asks: How does the papacy function so as to maintain its essence and meet contemporary needs? How does it take seriously the contributions of the voices of the People of God? How can it enter into meaningful dialogue with ecumenical partners? Though questions about how the papacy can balance concerns for unity and diversity in the church go to the heart of contemporary synodal conversations; they are not new. In fact, the nature of the papacy and the means for its renewal have been a subject of theological reflection throughout the church's history. John Paul II, for example, explored these questions in his encyclical on ecumenism, *Ut Unum Sint*. There he made a bold and ecumenically significant statement on the need to continuously renew the papacy:

> Whatever relates to the unity of all Christian communities clearly forms part of the concerns of the primacy. As Bishop of Rome, I am fully aware, as I have reaffirmed in the present Encyclical Letter, that Christ ardently desires the full and visible communion of all those Communities in which, by virtue of God's faithfulness, his Spirit dwells. I am convinced that I have a particular responsibility in this regard, above all in acknowledging the ecumenical aspirations of the majority of the Christian Communities and in heeding the request made of me *to find a way of exercising the primacy which, while in no way renouncing what is essential to its mission, is nonetheless open to a new situation.*[14]

While John Paul II's statement about the need to identify "a way of exercising the primacy" to meet "a new situation" is courageous and important, it is not especially innovative. Instead, it reminds us of the fact that the commitment to *Ecclesia semper reformanda* belongs as much to the papacy as to any other office or structure in the church. Approaches to

---

14. Pope John Paul II, Encyclical Letter *Ut Unum Sint* 95, May 25, 1995, https://www.vatican.va/content/john-paul-ii/en/encyclicals/documents/hf_jp-ii_enc_25051995_ut-unum-sint.html. Emphasis mine.

papal authority must be "open to a new situation" in order to preserve the health of the church, particularly as its listens to the voices of the People of God.[15]

In the "new situation" of an increasingly synodal church, the papacy should serve as a center that builds relationships and fosters listening among the faithful. The papacy must listen to diverse constituencies in the church representing wide expressions of the *sensus fidelium* and bring them together to discern how the Holy Spirit is speaking to the People of God. This conceivably includes outcomes of variegated unity or unity in diversity. Thus, the role of promoting unity should not be synonymous with promoting uniformity. A synodal papacy could support training and formation for listening as well as structures for feedback that direct the *sensus fidelium* in an upward motion that informs ecclesial teaching and governance. Other ways that a synodal papacy finds expression might include, for example, efforts to foster unity among Christians and reconciliation among divided churches, speaking on behalf of Christians worldwide on issues such as immigration or environmental degradation, gathering people for international events such as World Youth Day, and providing resources for protecting churches against intrusions by the state or religious discrimination. The pope can also be a bridge-builder in seeking to heal relationships among nations and between the church and the political realm or the church and society. These bridge-building and convening exercises of the Petrine ministry demonstrate

---

15. An excellent source for exploring the development of the papacy is Hermann J. Pottmeyer, *Towards a Papacy in Communion: Perspectives from Vatican Councils I & II* (New York: Herder and Herder, 1998). Pottmeyer wrote his book in response to John Paul II's call to find a new situation for the papacy, one which is rooted in the church's tradition. He examines the development of the papacy, demonstrating that it has looked different at different periods of history, to help us envision what it might look like in the future.

their roots in the witness of the Gospel, and their authenticity invites dialogue. None of this is to say that the juridical dimensions of the papal office should be abandoned as inauthentic. The pope's efforts to maintain unity and respond to the promptings of the Holy Spirit may necessarily unfold in juridical terms. The juridical exercise of papal authority often promotes unity by clarifying reliable pathways and offices for authentic listening. Nevertheless, in a synodal church, the juridical dimension of primacy necessarily seeks to facilitate a listening and bridge-building culture.[16]

Efforts to imagine and realize a bridge-building papacy come not only from theological reflection but from the actions and witness of the bishop of Rome. An example from ecumenical dialogue is illustrative. Between 2012 and 2017, I (Kristin) served as a member of the eighth round of the Roman Catholic Reformed Dialogue in the United States, which met to reflect on questions related to authority and ministry. In these discussions, as is often the case in ecumenical dialogue, the topic of the papacy presented a stumbling block. Some Reformed members expressed concern that the juridical authority of the papacy did not demonstrate consistency with the witness of Scripture and tradition. Particular and concrete exercises of papal authority gave the impression that unity in the Catholic Church was constituted by external bonds, such as submission to juridical structures and dictates, rather than by a dynamic, internal unity of the Spirit. Through years of committed dialogue, our group reached some areas of greater mutual understanding even as the topic of papal authority remained divisive.

In the midst of this dialogue, in September 2015, Pope Francis made a historic trip to the United States. During his

---

16. See Kristin Colberg, "Expanding Horizons 150 Years after Vatican I: Towards a Renewed Relationship between Synodality and Primacy," *Theological Studies* 83/1 (2022): 70–83.

visit, he eschewed many of the formal and ceremonial engagements that typically characterize such an official occasion and chose instead to spend time at a prison, an elementary school, and with the Little Sisters of the Poor. Francis's witness to the Gospel and Christ-like ministry moved some Reformed members of the dialogue so profoundly that they proposed that the dialogue team issue a statement about its impact. The statement read:

> As Reformed and Catholic participants in a long-standing official theological dialogue, we have been inspired by the ecumenical promise seen in the recent visit of Pope Francis to the United States. While the role of the Bishop of Rome has historically been a matter of contention between Reformed and Catholic communions, we affirm the manner in which Pope Francis modeled a service of unity for the whole church and its ministry. In his intentional compassion for those on society's margins, his pastoral visits with prisoners, his identification with immigrants, his care for the integrity of God's creation, and his public testimony to the values of the gospel, he gave voice and witness to aspirations of the wider Christian community. His servant heart gives hope for further developments along the road toward Christian unity, a journey that we trace to the Second Vatican Council and continue through our dialogue. Although we recognize that significant differences remain between us, we trust that the visit of Pope Francis will prompt further, honest dialogue—between our communions and others—in our search for a full expression of our unity in Christ.[17]

17. Adopted on October 6, 2015, at the 6th meeting of Round VIII of the official Roman Catholic-Reformed Dialogue in the United States, meeting at New Brunswick Seminary to discuss the topic of ecclesiology, https://www.usccb.org/beliefs-and-teachings/ecumenical-and-interreligious/ecumenical/reformed/upload/Roman-Catholic-Reformed-Statement-on-Pope-Francis-Visit.pdf.

Witnessing Francis's exercise of the Petrine ministry did not alleviate all of the ecumenical challenges associated with papal authority, but it shifted the way that our group approached this subject. The impact of the papal visit affirmed Paul VI's belief that modern men and women listen "more willingly to witnesses than to teachers, and if [they do] listen to teachers, it is because they are witnesses."[18] This insight highlights that some of the most effective moments of evangelization unfold when a person of faith gives authentic witness to the Gospel, which in turn prompts another person to ask, "Why do you live that way?" In this context, openness to dialogue becomes possible in new ways. Something similar happened in our dialogue. Reformed members of the dialogue team saw the example of Pope Francis and then asked their Catholic counterparts, "Can you tell us again about the role of the pope in your church?" This example demonstrates that advances in thinking about structures and offices come not only from developing compelling academic arguments but from witnessing encounters and events where structures and leaders embody true discipleship.

Synodalizing the church requires renewal on the level of universal structures. There is often a perception that structures in Rome are bureaucratic or institutional and, ultimately, inimical to the types of reforms demanded by synodality. When people seek to identify effective examples of ecclesial reform, they most often think of changes that emanated from efforts at the grassroots level. However, while it is true that prophetic voices in local communities feed ecclesial renewal, in a synodal church many of the most effective ecclesial reforms come from the center. Reforms initiated in Rome or within canon law can bring about quick change and find broad

---

18. Pope Paul VI, Apostolic Exhortation *Evangelii Nuntiandi* 4, December 8, 1975, https://www.vatican.va/content/paul-vi/en/apost_exhortations/documents/hf_p-vi_exh_19751208_evangelii-nuntiandi.html.

implementation. Reforms originating from the center needn't always be "centralizing reforms" aimed at deemphasizing local authority. Reforms originating at the center can also effect "diversifying reforms" that can make the church more diverse rather than more uniform. Such efforts often stimulate reform by providing space for decisions to be made locally or embracing what is already happening in a local community.

The Synod on Synodality itself is an example of a diversifying reform coming from the universal level. At the start of the synod, Pope Francis mandated that every diocese hold listening sessions with the goal of allowing the People of God to voice their diverse experiences of joys and needs within the church's life. This massive act of empowering voices at the grassroots level was the product of a decision made at "the center." This decision brought about chances for renewal in a faster and more comprehensive way than any local church or group of local churches could have achieved. Further, it allowed the church to listen in a way that was more participatory, dynamic, and diverse than at any other time in its history. Universal structures can catalyze a growth in synodal attitudes, practices, and relationships. They can be powerful instruments for listening and for setting the church "in motion" in ways that are in sync with the movement of the Spirit. In a synodalization of the church, its universal structures are not forgotten, nor do they lose their essence; instead they find a different style of expression.

Canon Law

Another crucial way that synodalization can be achieved at every level of the church's life is through a revision of canon law. We treat it separately here because canon law is not limited to any one level—local, regional, universal—but impacts all of them. A synodal update of the Code of Canon Law could have an immense and comprehensive impact on the church's life. Some perceive canon law as exceedingly technical and impersonal. The most common contact points for lay Catholics with canon law are typically the marriage tribunal and the annulment process. The fact that these points of contact can make the church seem legalistic at a time of crisis or loss has left many concerned with canon law's sterility and disconnection from the church's everyday pastoral life.

However, canon law offers a crucial tool for building synodality because it concretizes theological convictions in practical ways and holds the church accountable to its beliefs. *Accountability* is a key word in synodal understandings of church. For example, if the church believes in the *sensus fidei*, it should have structures, practices, and formation that call out the voices of the People of God. Further, it must ensure that it does not merely invite people to speak; it must also elucidate meaningful responses to what it has heard. Canon law ought to identify more moments where consultation of the faithful is vital or even required. Reforming canon law to suit the needs of a synodal church might include developing, and in some instances even requiring, processes of communal discernment in particular situations or at particular intervals. It might also include insisting upon diversity in the membership of parish councils to ensure that a wide range of voices would be heard. Canon law has a unique ability to hold the church accountable to its beliefs and to promote balance and mutuality among different expressions of authority such as the papacy, episcopal authority, and the *sensus fidelium* in order to call forth and discern "what the Spirit is saying to the churches."

Conclusion

This chapter has discussed a synodal transformation of structures at the local, regional, and universal levels. Such a transformation is not a matter of merely "rearranging furniture"; it represents a renewal of the whole church that comes from its deepest identity. It connects structures to the theological convictions underpinning synodality and wonders: How can structures help the whole church walk together and listen to the Spirit? An important issue in this synodal transformation of structures is to navigate several creative tensions, especially those between unity and diversity, Rome and the local churches, conservation and innovation, decision-making and decision-taking, and discernment and dialogue. Most importantly we need the virtue of patient expectation for mature solutions to emerge. While synodality does not begin or end in the reform of ecclesial structures, becoming a synodal church cannot be achieved without their renewal. One thing is certain: church structures are not boring, purely administrative, or theologically meaningless. Church structures tell us a great deal about who we are. They can serve as a powerful witness to our Christian identity, or they can provide an equally powerful counter-witness. A synodal church that honors the People of God as active agents who receive and transmit the word of God must manifest structures that involve the faithful in processes of discernment, planning, decision-making, and co-governance at all levels of the church's life.

Chapter Eight

The Power of Synodal Practices

Learning from the Benedictines

The previous chapters have explored two types of renewal and reform that are both crucially important for synodalizing the church, namely, first, personal conversion of attitudes and behavior and, second, structural reform of rules, procedures, and organization. Yet these cannot succeed without a third type of renewal, namely, that of ecclesial practices. As we discussed in chapter five, we need to acknowledge that our capacity for personal conversion is modest and that structural reforms cannot save us, for their impact remains limited. As human beings are essentially related to others and deeply marked by that, we need the power of habitual behavior of groups and communities to assist us in the process of adopting synodality as the church's standard way of proceeding. This chapter turns to a well-established example of such a practice, the Benedictine religious life, and explores what light it sheds on making synodality a constitutive ecclesial practice.

Both the *Instrumentum Laboris* 2023 and the subsequent Synthesis Report 2023 acknowledge that the consecrated life can be a helpful starting point for exploring how the church may become more synodal, as this way of life has for centuries been supported and strengthened in essential ways by processes of communal discernment, participatory governance, and mechanisms for listening. The Synthesis Report speaks of "the practices of synodal life and discernment that have been tried and tested in communities of consecrated life, maturing over the centuries," adding, "We know that we can learn from them wisdom in how to walk the synodal path."[1]

Encouraged by that conviction, in this chapter we zoom in on Benedictine wisdom. The Benedictine life is named after Saint Benedict of Nursia (480–550/60) and includes two major reformed branches, the Cistercians and Trappists. It takes the Rule of Saint Benedict as a guide for organizing a common life of prayer and work—*ora et labora*—under the leadership of an abbot or abbess. The *ora* is a major part of Benedictine life. Brothers or sisters gather various times a day to pray in common (what is called "the *opus Dei*," the work of God) but also have their personal prayer times, which typically include a particular form of Scripture meditation known as *lectio divina*. The *labora* means that brothers and sisters work to earn their living. For example, throughout history Benedictines have been major land developers, and these days Benedictines are known for their beers, cheese, meat, pottery, soap, schools, and so on.

Members of the Benedictine family point out that the synodal process has made them aware that their Rule and their way of life have much to offer in the development of a more synodal church. For example, Mauro-Giuseppe Lepori, abbot general of the Cistercian Order, commented in a letter to the order, "Ever since Pope Francis launched the synodal path, recalling that synodality is part of the nature of the church, I have been real-

---

1. Synthesis Report 2023, 10b. Note that it avoids idealizing the religious life and points out various kinds of abuse.

izing ever more clearly how much our Benedictine-Cistercian charism is marked by ecclesial synodality."[2] In what follows, we will highlight three key features of the Benedictine practice that are thoroughly synodal and which therefore might inspire a synodal church: first, life as a process of ongoing formation; second, multifaceted hierarchical, convincing, and pastoral leadership; and third, the role of regular and broad consultation.[3] Before concluding, we will broaden the perspective and suggest a few other possible sources of inspiration.

Monastic Life as a Formation Process

In the first place, formation is essential to Benedictine life. Monastic life is a never-ending learning process, aimed at leaving behind wayward attitudes and growing in faith, hope, and charity. Benedict speaks in the Prologue of his Rule about wanting to establish "a school for the Lord's service."[4] The goal of that school is to embrace a certain lifestyle (or *conversatio morum*), which is so important that it is one of the three vows that monks take.[5]

For Benedict, all monks must seek lifelong learning. That becomes very clear in the opening chapter of the Rule, in which Benedict lists two good types of monks, namely, those

2. Mauro-Giuseppe Lepori, OCist, "Synodality of Communion: Letter of the Abbot General for Pentecost 2022," https://www.ocist.org/ocist /images/pdf/ENPentecost2022.pdf.

3. The interpretation that follows is our own but has made use of Adalbert de Vogüé, OSB, *Reading Saint Benedict: Reflections on the Rule* (Kalamazoo, MI: Cistercian Publications, 1994).

4. Quotations from the Rule are taken from Benedict of Nursia, *RB 1980: The Rule of St. Benedict in English*, ed. Timothy Fry, OSB (Collegeville, MN: Liturgical Press, 1981), with occasional changes in light of the original Latin. Cf. the image of the monastery as a "workshop" (RB 4).

5. The Latin evokes conversion (*conversio*) but its meaning is debated; for the vows see RB 58.17, cf. Prol. 49 and RB 58.1.

who live under a rule and an abbot, and those who, having done so, have grown strong enough to continue the spiritual life (or "the battle," as Benedict has it) by themselves. These two types of monks he opposes with two other types of monks who either do what they like—"whatever strikes their fancy"—or who never settle down and wander from place to place (RB 1). The problem with these latter types of monks is that they avoid any formation process.[6]

Crucial for that learning process is the spiritual leadership of the abbot, whose role is so important that it is the subject of two chapters in the Rule (and in fact more). Equally crucial is the monk's openness to formation; a monk must want to receive instruction, feedback, and correction. The very opening words of the Rule highlight the importance of a receptive attitude: "Listen, my son [or daughter], to the master's instruction, and bend the ear of your heart." It translates into two key virtues for the monk: obedience (RB 5) and humility (RB 7). The latter is a technical term and means a profound ascetism of decentering from self to God, the superior, and the community, with growth in love and service as its ultimate aim.

In fact, that formation process is largely realized not through humble obedience to the abbot but through the common life. Modern commentators such as Abbot General Lepori underscore the formative value of a communal lifestyle. In his 2022 Pentecost reflection on synodality, he described living together as "a paschal transformation" of dying to self and rising to new life, as a community.[7] According to Lepori, this transforma-

---

6. On taking RB 1 as the starting point for a reflection on synodality, see Luca Fallica, OSB, "The Spiritual Experience of Saint Benedict and the Synodal Path of the Church," July 10, 2023, https://abbaziamontecassino .it/carisma/abate-di-montecassino-luca-fallicaspriritualita-benedettina-e -sinodo/. Fallica is the abbot of Montecassino (Italy), the first house of the Benedictine order, established by Benedict himself around 529.

7. Lepori, "Synodality of Communion."

tion is a key element of the Rule: "The whole Rule again and again proposes steps for growing in the life of communion, for passing therefore through death of our false, isolated 'I' to the paschal life of the 'I' in the ecclesial 'we.' "[8] A crucial element of that process is that "they shall bear one another's weaknesses of body and behavior with the utmost patience," as the chapter on the monk's "good zeal" notes (RB 72), although it is not limited to that. The chapter also speaks about honoring one's brothers as much as one can and even obeying one's brothers as much as one can. Here we see that, towards the end, the Rule develops into promoting a general attitude of charitable and humble interaction that serves the other and, therefore, the community.

Synodality Is Situated within the Church's Common Life

Thus, a first particularity of the Benedictine practice is that Benedictine life is very much about formation, which may be a painful process and which can only happen if one is willing to listen, learn, and grow in communion. How may this inspire and form a more synodal way of proceeding?

In the first place, Benedictine life helps to get the priorities right: we should not focus on decisions and outcomes. Synodality understood as shared decision-making is part of a much larger and much more significant project of journeying together. While monks share their views only occasionally—namely, when there is a chapter (or at the election of an abbot, or when they have been given an impossible task)—they rub shoulders every day. In the Benedictine project, the common life with its humdrum, joys, and tensions matters greatly; it is where

8. Here Lepori probably echoes words from the International Theological Commission's 2018 document *Synodality in the Life and Mission of the Church* 107.

our paschal transformation from *I* to *we* takes place. The means for that transformation are, in addition to the shared prayer, the concrete work, and tasks one may fulfill, simply living together in general and bearing with one another.

Highlighting the journey rather than the outcome—instead of imagining synodality with a narrow focus on shared decision-making—does not belittle the synodal endeavor but rather enlarges it. The ecclesial project in which shared decision-making has a place is one of fraternal living together and growing in mercy by bearing with one another. Abbot General Lepori goes as far as saying that a communion of this kind is the very core of the church's mission: "Fraternal communion in Christ is the substance of the mission, of the church's whole mission, including the mission of monasteries. Communion is the motive, the method, and the end; the origin, the meaning, and the purpose of the church's mission."[9] Here emerges the second particularity of a Benedictine approach, namely, that a good part of our formation process into a community does not need to be organized; it is simply there in the form of our living together as a faith community with very diverse characters and gifts. For our diversity to become formative, it should not be suppressed but embraced.

This sheds a particular light on the need for formation addressed in the official documents for the synod. In light of the Benedictine tradition, it is important to underline that this formation is not the usual catechetical formation; it is *personal* formation. It is not just the transmission of information but a capacity to appreciate each person's gifts and, if that is not possible, charitably bear with one another. As it is a paschal formation, it will involve making space for others and, in a certain sense, dying to self.

---

9. Lepori, "Synodality of Communion."

To help us develop the practice of journeying together, the Synod 2021–24 process suggests things that we can do and that may benefit us. Our sense of journeying together is greatly enhanced by meeting one another and spending time together, in the formal setting of round table conversations as much as in the informal setting of coffee breaks or drinks. Even the fact that the synod participants were going on a short retreat *together* forms part of it. Some Synod 2023 participants suggested sharing more meals together, which would be another possibility. Could similar community-building activities be developed in parishes and dioceses? Have we sometimes become too focused on sacraments and too efficient in meetings? Should we spend more time together?

The Abbot's Multifaceted Leadership

Second, Benedictine practice is characterized by a strong yet multifaceted leadership. Several chapters of the Rule elaborate what that leadership should look like, especially RB 2 and 64 on the abbot, RB 21 on the deans, RB 31 on the cellarer, and RB 65 on the prior. In line with the tradition of the desert fathers and mothers, this leadership has a strong vertical dimension and is located particularly in the abbot. For example, we read in RB 2 that the abbot "is believed to hold the place of Christ in the monastery," and that the relationship between the abbot and the monks is that of a teacher and students (or *discipuli*). In the chapter on obedience, the Rule specifies that monks are supposed to carry out with prompt obedience whatever the superior orders (RB 5), which echoes the tradition of the desert fathers and desert mothers according to which the assignments of one's master are to be followed without questioning, even if absurd. When other leadership roles are discussed, Benedict always recalls that those, too, have the abbot as their point of reference.

Interestingly, however, that is not the full story, as the abbot's leadership has various other dimensions also, so that it is best described as multifaceted. For a start, the abbot's leadership is clearly situated under God, who will call the abbot to account for his leadership of the community, as the Rule repeats at various instances. RB 2 and RB 64 both point out that the abbot cannot invent his own rules and should stick to the Gospel. The Rule—or even "holy Rule" (RB 65)— constitutes another limitation of the abbot's power, or rather, the framework for his leadership.

In the second place, the abbot is supposed to lead an exemplary spiritual and moral life. The opening line of RB 2 recalls that "the abbot who is worthy of governing a monastery must always remember what his title signifies and verify the name of superior [*maior*] by his actions."[10] One should live up to one's role. According to the Rule, an abbot teaches both by words and by actions, with the latter being stressed: "He must point out to them all that is good and holy more by actions than by words" (RB 2.11–15). These same points structure the chapter on the election of the abbot (RB 64). After stating that he "shall be chosen for the merit of his life and the wisdom of his teaching," with no consideration of his rank in the community, the chapter details a long list of actions to be avoided and virtues to be embraced. Here we are far removed from a purely vertical culture; Benedictine leadership needs to be convincing. As the abbot can only expect something from his subjects when he himself lives virtuously, he needs conversion just like his brothers do.

---

10. The Latin words are evocative. Abbot comes from the Latin *abbas*, evoking both the Aramaic *abba* ("father") and the desert fathers and mothers who were called abba and amma. It has a fatherly, caring sound. Superior is the translation of *maior*, which sounds like older and wiser companion and echoes the *geron* (old man, meaning, experienced wise person), again from the wisdom tradition from the desert.

Thirdly, in his leadership the abbot should pay attention to the character, capacities, and situation of each person and adapt his treatment accordingly. The words of the Rule sound surprisingly modern: "The abbot must vary with circumstances, threatening and coaxing by turns, stern as a master, tender as a father," and "he must so accommodate and adapt himself to each one's character and intelligence that he will not only keep the flock entrusted to his care from dwindling, but will rejoice in the increase of a good flock" (RB 2).[11] A later chapter explicitly states that material goods should *not* be given equally to everybody. Quoting the Scripture verse "distribution was made to every one according to his needs" (Acts 4:35), Benedict states that people's "weaknesses" should be considered (RB 34). This means that in some cases the abbot should push someone to take the next step or clearly correct someone, and in other cases he should be lenient and mild (RB 2). Note that this involves details like the bedding that a monk is given (RB 22), as well as the food and drink each one receives (RB 39–40)! Much of this accommodating leadership is summed up in the brief note that the abbot should be loved more than feared (RB 64).

The point of this type of leadership is pastoral and spiritual: to help people go forward. Benedictine wisdom suggests that the leader needs to find the right balance between challenging people to make headway and moderating his comments to avoid discouragement or exhaustion (RB 64). Even corrections are understood within this perspective: in punishing monks,

---

11. Commentators point out that in introducing this point, Benedict takes a noticeably different approach than the Rule of the Master, the sixth-century text to which he is heavily indebted. Cf. de Vogüé, *Reading Saint Benedict*, 48–49, commenting on RB 2.23–29: "In fact, his [Benedict's] addition is the exact opposite of the passage he eliminated [from the example of the Rule of the Master]: far from acting in identical fashion towards all, the abbot is again exhorted to vary his conduct."

the abbot is compared to "a wise physician" who seeks remedies to heal (RB 27–28). Benedictine leadership may, therefore, be described as contextual or pastoral leadership and is, once again, far removed from a purely vertical leadership.

Finally, the abbot is not alone to rule the monastery. The Rule specifies various other leadership roles, such as the deans of the monastery, the cellarer, and the prior. Deans are those with whom the abbot of a big monastery may "share his burden" as they overlook smaller groups of monks (RB 21–23). The cellarer takes care of material things (RB 31), and the prior is the assistant superior (RB 65). While the Rule recalls that they should heed the orders of the abbot—something which is elaborated especially for the prior—it is also clear that they have their own responsibilities. Especially in the extensive description of the cellarer's role, one hears echoes of the contextual, pastoral, spiritual leadership of the abbot. For example, "If a brother should present him with an unreasonable request, [the cellarer] shall not give him cause for sadness by rejecting him with contempt, but he shall humbly answer the improper request with a reasonable refusal" (RB 31).

Humble, Convincing, and Pastoral Leadership

Thus, a second particularity of the Benedictine way of proceeding is its multifaceted leadership. Benedictine life underlines the crucial importance of leadership while also shifting the focus away from power. While there is no doubt about the abbot's authority, it is not absolute; rather, it is situated under God. Meant to serve each monk's personal growth, it should be flexible. Moreover, it should be convincing and therefore the abbot should live by what he teaches others. Finally, the abbot can share the burden of his leadership with others if need be. How may each of these facets inspire and form a more synodal practice in the church?

The key concern of Benedictine leadership seems to be the spiritual growth of each of the members of the community and that of the community as a whole. Or, in negative terms, the key concern is *not* dogmatic, as in defending orthodoxy, or managerial, as in "running" parishes or the diocese. This suggests that ecclesial leadership should prioritize the spiritual life of the faithful, which requires a contextual and flexible approach that stands out for its moderation, mercy, and wisdom. Instead of making all-or-nothing dogmatic or ethical orthodoxy their primary concern, leaders should opt primarily for a pastoral style of nearness and accompaniment. While conservative circles may fear that such a pastoral flexibility will destroy the church, for Benedict the point is the exact opposite: it helps people to progress as they can. The Rule's outlook is both very pragmatic and deeply spiritual: "The abbot must so arrange everything that the strong may have something to yearn for and the weak nothing to run from" (RB 64). As such, it is a way of building up a church that journeys together with each and every person at their own pace.

That requires a convincing leadership. Moral integrity and spiritual wisdom should be key criteria for leaders. The "shepherds" should be living witnesses of the paschal formation process that their "sheep" are called to. The spiritual and ethical authenticity of practicing what they preach will both dispel the fear that they are watering down things and make them convincing leaders. To avoid haughty leadership, leaders should withstand clerical impulses and remind themselves that God is the deepest ground of ecclesial realities. To become humble leaders, it can be helpful to observe that, although the Rule compares the abbot to Christ, he is not himself the ultimate leader; he is directed (or "ruled") by the Rule and is reminded that God will call him to account.

To help us develop a practice of a humble, convincing, and pastoral leadership practice, much work needs to be done. Something as unspectacular as actual contact with the People of God seems to be the most important "exercise," as it invites leaders to come down from clerical pedestals and to leave theoretical bubbles. When one encounters people as they are, one is both impressed by their virtues—which calls leaders to imitate them—and touched by their troubles—which calls leaders to pastoral attitudes of mercy and adaptation. Here the Synthesis Report speaks helpful words. It calls priests and deacons to create bonds of closeness and synodal attitudes "from the earliest stages of formation by ensuring close contact with the People of God and through concrete service-learning experiences among those most in need."[12] This would also apply to bishops. Speaking of the latter, the Synthesis Report specifies that "his ministry is realized in a synodal manner when governance is accompanied by co-responsibility, preaching by listening to the faithful People of God, and sanctification and celebration of the liturgy by humility and conversion."[13] Co-responsibility ties in well with the fact that, in Benedictine governance, the abbot does not fulfill all the leadership roles by himself but clearly shares responsibility; that is a key element for a synodal church also.

To conclude this section, let us signal the practical nature of what we are proposing here. With its model of ministry rooted in community and service, the Benedictine tradition can help us synodalize ecclesial practices, offering a helpful alternative to exclusively hierarchical ways of proceeding. Theologians can support this by continuing the effort to reimagine the theology of ministry in such a way that a sacralized, cultic priesthood, which stresses difference, is replaced by one that is rooted in the community and in service of the variety of charismatic gifts in the community.

The Views of the Monks Matter

A third characteristic of Benedictine practice is that the views of the monks play an important role in the life of the

12. Synthesis Report 2023, 11c.
13. Synthesis Report 2023, 12b.

community. The Rule identifies various moments in which they share their views, all of which further situate the abbot's leadership.

Firstly, the monks play a major role in choosing their own leader. Different from earlier monastic traditions, according to which abbots appointed their successors, here the community elects its own leader.[14] Although Benedict is not very clear about the details of that election, he is clear about what the community should look for in a leader. "The one to be ordained [i.e., elected abbot] shall be chosen for the merit of his life and the wisdom of his teaching, even if he ranks last in the community" (RB 64). The criterion is not one's place in the monastery's hierarchy, which is based on the time spent in the monastery, but spiritual leadership qualities.

The Rule also gives great weight to the views of the monks when important decisions are being made. The chapter on the abbot (RB 2) is immediately followed by the chapter on "summoning the brothers for counsel" (RB 3), the point of which is summarized well by Gregory Polan, abbot primate of the Benedictine order: "It is clear that for Benedict, important major decisions affecting the entire community's well-being were to be made by the community as a whole."[15]

For this to function well, the Rule specifies the following. The abbot should clearly explain what is at stake (to which modern commentators add that he needs to create a safe atmosphere

---

14. See de Vogüé, *Reading Saint Benedict*, 299–300: "Benedict's system of succession is completely different [than that of the Rule of the Master]. The former abbot has no part in it at all. It is up to the community to choose its leader."

15. Gregory J. Polan, OSB, "Synodal Elements in the Rule of St. Benedict," *The American Benedictine Review* 73 (2022): 2. This article is a revised version of Polan, "Benedictine Spirituality," https://www.synod.va/content/dam /synod/common/resources/spirituality/benedict/EN_Spiri_Polan.pdf.

that invites all community members to speak).[16] He should listen to the view of the brothers. In doing so, he should have a special interest in the views of the young ones, as "the Lord often reveals what is better to the younger." The brothers for their part should speak without insisting on their point of view and without putting pressure by speaking in the name of others or a group. What the monks present should simply be their own point of view. It is supposed that these points of view are the fruit of prayerful reflection rather than one's own design. Finally, the abbot should ponder what was said and make a final decision, which monks should accept.

In the Rule, the participation of the monks remains limited to sharing their views; once the consultation is done, the abbot ponders and decides. Yet modern commentators stretch the role of the community and make consultation a dialogical undertaking, to the point of sometimes speaking of "communal listening and discernment."[17] Thus, the counsel at the very beginning of the Rule to "bend the ear of your heart" characterizes not only the monk's readiness to learn from the abbot but also the readiness of all to learn from one another, and even that of the abbot to learn from the monks. As Willekes puts it, "The type of meeting Benedict intends is not so much about what I may want to say, but rather what I may hear. Or even, what the Lord wants me to hear and, thereby, to reveal to me."[18] Prior to the abbot taking a decision and the monks following that decision, the monks may learn from one another and as a community journey to a decision.

---

16. As American Benedictine sister Jennifer Mechtild Horner states, he should "create a safe space where one can speak and be heard and where differences are embraced rather than being feared." Jennifer Horner, OSB, "Listening with the Ear of the Heart: The Rule of Benedict and Synodality," *Monastic Bulletin* 123 (2022): 26.

17. Horner, "Listening with the Ear of the Heart," 26.

18. Willekes, "Synodal Wisdom from the Rule of Benedict," 8.

A third example of the monk being invited to (or at least allowed to) share his voice can be found in the chapter on the question of what to do "if impossible tasks are assigned to a brother" (RB 68). Echoing RB 3, on the consultation of the brothers, the chapter recommends humbly bringing the matter to the attention of one's superior, who then decides. Benedict opts for a realistic obedience rather than ascetically idealizing and absolutizing obedience.[19] Maybe this suggests a more general possibility to speak one's mind with the superior, too. Elsewhere, the Rule recommends great transparency towards the abbot concerning one's sins and inner life.[20] Does this include sharing one's views of how things are going in the monastery?

Thus, the Rule gives ample space for the monks to share their view of God's will, as they best see it, without downplaying the role of the abbot. The monks elect the abbot, contribute their views when important matters are considered, and can speak up when things are too difficult for them. The abbot's leadership remains yet is complemented—informed, enriched, questioned, corrected—by these other elements. The basic presupposition in all of this is that God's will may be communicated through others than the abbot. Willekes speaks of "two forms of wisdom": young monks with little experience may refresh the wisdom of the experienced monks, who say more traditional things.[21] She points out that, according to Benedict, even outsiders may say useful things (RB 61)! Beyond an act of humility on the part of the abbot—humility being the great virtue of monasticism—listening to the views of the monks is primarily meant to better hear God's voice.

19. De Vogüé points out that in so doing, Benedict opts for a very different approach than the desert tradition and than the Rule of the Master. See de Vogüé, *Reading Saint Benedict*, 317–19.

20. RB 7 speaks about transparency concerning "any evil thoughts entering our hearts or any evil deeds committed in secret."

21. Willekes, "Synodal Wisdom from the Rule of Benedict," 8.

Faithful Who Speak, Leaders Who Listen

In allowing monks to vote and to speak their mind, Benedictine practice operates with the humble awareness that a brother or sister may offer wisdom in God's name. What could this mean for a synodal church? In the first place, the general principle is worth considering: the faithful may actually say useful things that help the church forward; insight and wisdom are not the privilege of leaders. A more synodal church is called to adopt a more positive view of the contributions of the laity, deacons, priests, and religious.

In addition, the Benedictine example calls ecclesial leaders and the faithful to engage in a new style of conversation. As we have seen, the Rule is quite particular about how the monks should speak and the abbot should listen. Can faithful men and women grow in the art of speaking their mind and explaining their point succinctly, without anger, frustration, or pressure, and without trying to win over the other person? Can leaders grow in the art of listening and pondering before actually deciding? It seems an understatement to say that both groups can grow in the attitudes indicated here.

Finally, these two more general points—on a culture of trust and a cultivated style of conversing—should be "incarnated" in concrete procedures and specific topics for which the voice of the faithful (including deacons and priests) is taken seriously. The obvious examples are the nomination of bishops and major pastoral decisions in dioceses and parishes. Could it also include reflection on hot-button moral or dogmatic issues?

To help us develop these practices of speaking well and listening well, the Synod 2021–24 promoted spiritual conversation, or conversation in the Spirit, which was presented in chapter three of this book. The Benedictine practice of holding chapters and its modern interpretation as common discernment confirms the value of careful speaking and listening and thus journeying together. In both cases, the method is not its own goal but an instrument for creating communion: "This spiritual practice enables us to move from the 'I' to the 'we': it does not lose sight of or erase the personal dimension of the 'I,' but recognises it and inserts it into the community dimension."[22] Testimonies suggest that it worked well in the synod gatherings and that it created a new culture of listening and being together. For example, the Synthesis Report says, "The practice [of conversation in the Spirit] has elicited joy, awe and gratitude and has been experienced as a path of renewal that transforms individuals, groups, and the church."[23]

Yet spiritual conversation is certainly not the only way to practice speaking and listening well, and it should be complemented by a respectful style of going about arguments, something that spiritual conversation in its current form does not allow for.[24] Moreover, it seems useful to integrate elements from this spiritual conversation approach into other types of meetings that are not in themselves spiritual, such as board meetings, planning commissions, strategic boards, and so on. Without these meetings being transformed into spiritual sharing, they could adopt elements of it, such as spending some time on making up one's mind before speaking or inviting another participant with a different viewpoint to say more instead of offering a quick "yes, but" response. Possibilities for training the People of God in this method are vast and even include our normal day to day-to-day conversations.

From Whom Else May We Learn?

When the synod recommended that the church learn from "the practices of synodal life and discernment that have been tried and tested in communities of consecrated life, maturing

22. *Instrumentum Laboris* 2023, 35.
23. Synthesis Report 2023, 2d.
24. The Synthesis Report 2023 hints at this also, see 2j.

over the centuries,"[25] it spoke in the plural. The plural is well chosen, for the consecrated life offers a rich variety of practices. With the above therefore being no more than one case study, who else may we learn from, apart from the Benedictines?

Very different from the Benedictine tradition, the Dominican way of doing things is marked by a culture of conversation, searching for the truth, and doing so by relying on arguments rather than authorities. Because of human differences, pursuing truth and remaining in unity is a challenge. Speaking on Dominican spirituality and synodality, Timothy Radcliffe aptly noted, "The typically Protestant temptation is to champion truth at the expense of unity. The Catholic weakness is to insist on unity to the detriment of fearlessly seeking the truth. Both are premature resolutions of a tension that will always and necessarily abide."[26] He explains that we need bearing with one another, friendship, time, and patience. Can the Dominican tradition enlighten the church in this regard?[27]

To take one more example, the Jesuit way of proceeding is marked by power concentrated in the figure of the superior that recalls the vertical dimension that we also found in the Benedictine tradition. It has resulted in popular representations of the Jesuits as a military order with blind obedience. At the same time, the superior's power is strongly relativized, as Jesuit practice is marked by a culture of discernment. Before taking decisions, the superior should *discern* those decisions. Rather than following his own instincts or preferences, he should ask two questions: Does a possible decision come with an aftertaste of spiritual joy, peace, clarity, and so on?

---

25. Synthesis Report 2023, 10b.

26. Radcliffe, "Accountability and Co-Responsibility," 597.

27. Other elements of the Dominican charisms are a focus on being brothers, flexible constitutions, and voting. See Radcliffe, "Accountability and Co-Responsibility"; and Mangnus, "Dominican Gifts for a Synodal Church."

And if so, does it serve the greater good (or, if you prefer, the kingdom of God)? Moreover, as part of that discernment he should consult people, both in the form of a board of advisors (the so-called consult) and through a yearly confidential conversation with every Jesuit within his province.[28] Thus, Jesuit practice is multifaceted also.

It is easy to multiply examples. On July 1, 2021, synod participants experienced a day of reflection on synodal spiritualities, with presentations on Augustinian, Benedictine, Dominican, Sant'Egidio, Franciscan, Ignatian, Salesian, and Focolare perspectives.[29] (One may ask if young groups such as Sant'Egidio and Focolare have matured sufficiently to be included among such traditions.) Distinctively feminine traditions, such as that of the Ursuline sisters, would have further enriched the variety of perspectives.[30] Thus, in creating a synodal practice, we do not need to start from scratch; our tradition offers many existing models. They are best understood as *produktive Vorbilde*: examples that encourage and inspire to find one's own feet.

For doing that, the religious traditions are not the only resource. As we noted earlier, the Latin American and Caribbean bishops have ample experience with collaborating effectively at the continental level. Interestingly, pastors and theologians have usually played a role in those deliberations.

28. See Benoît Malvaux, SJ, "Le pouvoir délibératif dans la compagnie de Jésus: la lettre et l'esprit," in *Délibérer en Église*, ed. Alphonse Borras, 89–110 (Brussels: Lessius, 2010); and Moons, "Synodality and Discernment."

29. They were published under the "Spiritual and Liturgical Resources" at synod.va but not much note has been taken of these documents. See the links under "Synodal Spirituality" at https://www.synod.va/en/resources/spiritual-and-liturgical-resources.html.

30. Laure Blanchon, OSU, and Armida Veglio, OSU, "An Ursuline Perspective of Synodality," in *Witnesses of Synodality*, ed. Moons, 39–52.

More recently, as we saw in chapter seven, they have experimented with a new form, an "ecclesial assembly," with ample lay participation, rather than an episcopal conference (CELAM) assembly, which involves the participation of bishops almost exclusively.[31] What can their experience of collaboration and consultation teach the church? More recent examples, such as the Australian plenary council and the German *Synodaler Weg*, have perhaps not yet fully matured but may be worth consideration also.

To those we could further add cultural resources, such as the African palaver tradition, which is related to the notion of Ubuntu and which highlights the importance of the community in resolving issues.[32] India has a similar tradition, called Palliyogam.[33] Secular expertise from the world of organizational management may help also. The fact that participative leadership has become standard language says enough: most modern managers work with ample consultation, as this leads to better decisions and greater staff involvement in the process.

Conclusion

This chapter has highlighted the power of practices and, in so doing, has broadened the range of elements that are necessary for synodalizing the church. In addition to the subjective dimension of personal conversion and commitment to specific types of behavior (chapter six) and the objective dimension

---

31. See Weiler, "Synodality in a Continental Perspective," 134–36.

32. See, e.g., Stan Chu Ilo, "The African Palaver Method: A Model Synodal Process for Today's Church," *Concilium* (2021/2): 68–76; and Anna Arabome, SSS, "Synodality through an African Lens: Palaver and Ubuntu," in *Witnesses of Synodality*, ed. Moons, 118–30.

33. See Paul Pulikkan, "Learning from Different Synodal Experiences (Council of Aparecida, Der Synodale Weg, Querida Amazonia, and Palliyogam)," *Encounter* 12 (2021): 41–58.

of the reform of structures (chapter seven), we need to address the communitarian dimension. Synodalizing the church requires habits and ways of proceeding that effectively realize synodality. Not unlike how a novice is formed for the religious life by immersion, the People of God familiarizes itself with synodality by copying what others are doing and by "simply" following their example. The Benedictine tradition offers an instructive example of such a practice.

Realistically speaking, however, a synodal way of proceeding is not yet the church's standard practice. Ironically, therefore, before we can rely on synodal habits, we first need to consciously and deliberately adopt them—not unlike training. In that training, specific methods such as spiritual conversation function like exercises. Importantly, we should not underestimate the role each and every person can play, for anybody who listens well, speaks well, waits and ponders, and journeys together contributes to building up a synodal practice. Structures play an important role also.

———

To sum up this book, we have first looked at the theology and history of synodality, particularly as it has been unfolding over the past several years (part one), and then presented several elements that are crucial for continuing to "synodalize" the church as it moves into the future (part two). Clearly the journey is far from over. Instead of being discouraged by what has not yet been achieved, this book has highlighted the rich resources that are available in terms of theology, history, and encouraging examples.

To that we would like to add our personal experience. In our own involvement in the synodal journey, we have encountered the grace and power of synodality. This includes meeting many generous people who are committed to adopting more synodal ways of proceeding at a personal level and to promoting a more synodal structure when possible. Thus, the church has many resources at its disposal to learn from and to draw on as it seeks to journey together into the future. That consolation seems a fitting way to end this book.

Appendix 1

A Timeline of Key Events of the Synod 2021–2024

2021–2022   Diocesan Stage

Publication of the Preparatory Document and the *Vademecum* to explain and guide the synodal journey

Official opening of the Synod with an ecumenical prayer vigil and a Eucharist in Saint Peter's Basilica, Vatican City (October 9–10, 2021)

Local consultations, leading to national syntheses, sent to Rome in late spring 2022

2022–2023   Continental Stage

Frascati process (September 2022) to distill the national synthesis into a single document, leading to the publication of the Document for the Continental Stage

Continental gatherings, leading to the publication of the Final Documents of the Continental Assemblies

2023–2024   Universal Phase

Publication of the *Instrumentum Laboris* for the First Session

Synod of Bishops (October 2023), leading to the Synthesis Report

Publication of the *Instrumentum Laboris* for the Second Session

Synod of Bishops (October 2024), leading to, we anticipate, some form of a synthesis report and possibly a papal apostolic exhortation

Appendix 2

A Timeline of Key Documents in Relation to the Synod 2021–2024

2015

October 17   Pope Francis, Ceremony Commemorating the 50th Anniversary of the Institution of the Synod of Bishops

2018

March 2   International Theological Commission, Synodality in the Life and Mission of the Church

September 15   Pope Francis, Apostolic Constitution on the Synod of Bishops *Episcopalis Communio*

2021

September 7   General Secretariat for the Synod, Preparatory Document

September 7   General Secretariat for the Synod, *Vademecum* for the Synod on Synodality: Official Handbook for Listening and Discernment in Local Churches

September 18   Pope Francis, Address to the Faithful of the Diocese of Rome

October 9   Pope Francis, Address on the Occasion of the Moment of Reflection for the Beginning of the Synodal Journey

October 10   Pope Francis, Homily at the Opening of the Synodal Path

2022

October 27   General Secretariat for the Synod, Working Document for the Continental Stage

2023

Spring   Final Documents of the Continental Assemblies (Africa and Madagascar, Asia, Europe, Middle East, North America, Latin America and Caribbean, Oceania; also: Digital Synod)

June 20   General Secretariat for the Synod, *Instrumentum Laboris* for the First Session

October 29   General Secretariat for the Synod, Synthesis Report: A Synodal Church in Mission

2024

July 9   General Secretariat for the Synod, *Instrumentum Laboris* for the Second Session

October 26   Final Document of the XVI Assembly, For a Synodal Church: Communion, Participation, Mission

Select Bibliography

Official Church Documents and Papal Addresses, Letters, and Homilies

Acta Synodalia Sacrosancti Concililii Oecumenici Vaticani II. 32 vols. Vatican City: Typis Polyglottis Vaticanis, 1970–99.

Francis, Pope. Address at the Opening of the Synod of Bishops on Young People, the Faith and Vocational Discernment. October 3, 2018. https://www.vatican.va/content/francesco/en/speeches /2018/october/documents/papa-francesco_20181003_apertura-sinodo.html.

Francis, Pope. Address to the Faithful of the Diocese of Rome. September 18, 2021. https://www.vatican.va/content/francesco/ en/speeches/2021/september/documents/20210918-fedeli -diocesiroma.html.

Francis, Pope. Apostolic Constitution *Episcopalis Communio*. September 15, 2018. https://www.vatican.va/content/francesco/en /apost_constitutions/documents/papa-francesco_costituzione -ap_20180915_episcopalis-communio.html.

Francis, Pope. Apostolic Exhortation *Evangelii Gaudium*. November 24, 2013. https://www.vatican.va/content/francesco/en/apost _exhortations/documents/papa-francesco_esortazione-ap_2013 1124_evangelii-gaudium.html.

Francis, Pope. Ceremony Commemorating the 50th Anniversary of the Institution of the Synod of Bishops. October 17, 2015. https://www.vatican.va/content/francesco/en/speeches/2015 /october/documents/papa-francesco_20151017_50-anniversario -sinodo.html.

Francis, Pope. Greeting of Pope Francis to the Synod Fathers during the First General Congregation of the Third Extraordinary General Assembly of the Synod of Bishops. October 6, 2014. https://www.vatican.va/content/francesco/en/speeches/2014/october/documents/papa-francesco_20141006_padri-sinodali.html.

Francis, Pope. Homily: Conclusion of the Ordinary General Assembly of the Synod of Bishops. October 29, 2023. https://www.vatican.va/content/francesco/en/homilies/2023/documents/20231029-omelia-conclusione-sinodo.html.

Francis, Pope. Intervention of the Holy Father at the 18th General Congregation of the 16th Ordinary General Assembly of the Synod of Bishops. October 25, 2023. https://www.vatican.va/content/francesco/en/speeches/2023/october/documents/20231025-intervento-sinodo.html.

Francis, Pope. Morning Meditation: The Water Flowing through the Church. November 9, 2013. https://www.vatican.va/content/francesco/en/cotidie/2013/documents/papa-francesco-cotidie_20131109_water-flowing.html.

Francis, Pope. Presentation of the Christmas Greetings to the Roman Curia. December 22, 2014. https://www.vatican.va/content/francesco/en/speeches/2014/december/documents/papa-francesco_20141222_curia-romana.html.

General Secretariat for the Synod. *Instrumentum Laboris* for the 16th Ordinary General Assembly of the Synod of Bishops. June 20, 2023. https://press.vatican.va/content/salastampa/en/bollettino/pubblico/2023/06/20/230620e.html.

General Secretariat for the Synod. *Instrumentum Laboris* for the Second Session of the 16th Ordinary General Assembly of the Synod of Bishops. July 9, 2024. https://www.synod.va/en/news/the-instrumentum-laboris.html.

General Secretariat for the Synod. Preparatory Document: For a Synodal Church: Communion, Participation, Mission. September 7, 2021. https://www.synod.va/en/news/the-preparatory-document.html.

General Secretariat for the Synod. *Vademecum* for the Synod on Synodality. September 7, 2021. https://www.synod.va/en/news/the-vademecum-for-the-synod-on-synodality.html.

General Secretariat for the Synod. Working Document for the Continental Stage, Enlarge the Space of Your Tent. https://www.synod.va/en/highlights/working-document-for-the-continental-stage.html.

International Theological Commission. *Sensus Fidei* in the Life of the Church. 2014. https://www.vatican.va/roman_curia/congregations/cfaith/cti_documents/rc_cti_20140610_sensus-fidei_en.html.

International Theological Commission. Synodality in the Life and Mission of the Church. March 2, 2018. https://www.vatican.va/roman_curia/congregations/cfaith/cti_documents/rc_cti_20180302_sinodalita_en.html.

John Paul II, Pope. Encyclical Letter *Ut Unum Sint*. May 25, 1995. https://www.vatican.va/content/john-paul-ii/en/encyclicals/documents/hf_jp-ii_enc_25051995_ut-unum-sint.html.

Paul IV, Pope. Apostolic Exhortation *Evangelii Nuntiandi*. December 8, 1975. https://www.vatican.va/content/paul-vi/en/apost_exhortations/documents/hf_p-vi_exh_19751208_evangelii-nuntiandi.html.

Second Vatican Ecumenical Council. *Vatican Council II: Constitutions, Decrees, Declarations; The Basic Sixteen Documents*. Edited by Austin Flannery, OP. Collegeville, MN: Liturgical Press, 2014.

XVI Ordinary General Assembly of the Synod of Bishops. Synthesis Report: A Synodal Church in Mission. 2023. https://www.synod.va/content/dam/synod/assembly/synthesis/english/2023.10.28-ENG-Synthesis-Report.pdf.

Academic and Pastoral Resources

Alberigo, Giuseppe, and Joseph Komonchak, eds. *History of Vatican II*. 5 vols. Maryknoll, NY: Orbis, 1995–2003.

Allen Jr., John. "Just How Valuable Is Sitting at Round Tables?" *Catholic Herald*. October 28, 2023. https://catholicherald.co.uk/just-how-valuable-is-sitting-around-tables.

Arabome, Anna. "Synodality through an African Lens: Palaver and Ubuntu." In *Witnesses of Synodality: Good Practices and Experiences*, edited by Jos Moons, 118–30. Mahwah, NJ: Paulist Press, 2024.

Arenas, Sandra. "The Awakening of Chile: Demands for Participation and the Synodal Church." *Louvain Studies* 45 (2022): 97–111.

Becquart, Nathalie, and Philipp Renczes, eds. *Theology Responding to the Challenge of Synodality: Proceedings of International Conference Held at the Pontifical Gregorian University (Rome, 27–29 April 2023)*. Rome: Libreria Editrice Vaticana, 2024.

Benedict of Nursia. *RB 1980: The Rule of St. Benedict in English.* Edited by Timothy Fry. Collegeville, MN: Liturgical Press, 1981.

Blanchon, Laure, and Armida Veglio. "An Ursuline Perspective of Synodality." In *Witnesses of Synodality: Good Practices and Experiences*, edited by Jos Moons, 39–52. Mahwah, NJ: Paulist Press, 2024.

Borghesi, Massimo. *The Mind of Pope Francis: Jorge Mario Bergoglio's Intellectual Journey.* Translated by Barry Hudock. Collegeville, MN: Liturgical Press, 2018.

Borras, Alphonse. "Ecclesial Synodality, Participatory Processes, and Decision-Making Procedures: A Canonist's Point of View." In *For a Missionary Reform of the Church: The* Civiltà Cattolica *Seminar*, edited by Antonio Spadaro and Carlos Maria Galli, 218–48. Mahwah, NJ: Paulist Press, 2017.

Burkhard, John. "*Sensus Fidei*: Recent Theological Reflection (1990–2001) Part I." *The Heythrop Journal* 46 (2005): 450–75.

Burkhard, John. "*Sensus Fidei*: Recent Theological Reflection (1990–2001) Part II." *The Heythrop Journal* 47 (2006): 38–54.

Burkhard, John. "*Sensus Fidei*: Theological Reflection Since Vatican II: I.1965–84." *The Heythrop Journal* 34 (1993): 41–59, 123–36.

Clifford, Catherine, and Stephen Lampe, eds. *Vatican II at 60: Re-Energizing the Renewal.* Maryknoll, NY: Orbis, 2024.

Colberg, Kristin. "Expanding Horizons 150 Years after Vatican I: Towards a Renewed Relationship between Synodality and Primacy." *Theological Studies* 83/1 (2022): 70–83.

Colberg, Kristin. *Vatican I and Vatican II: Councils in the Living Tradition.* Collegeville, MN: Liturgical Press, 2016.

Cozzens, Donald. *Sacred Silence: Denial and the Crisis in the Church.* Collegeville, MN: Liturgical Press, 2004.

de Mey, Peter. "Church Renewal and Reform in the Documents of Vatican II: History, Theology, Terminology." *The Jurist* 71 (2011): 369–400.

de Vogüé, Adalbert. *Reading Saint Benedict: Reflections on the Rule.* Kalamazoo, MI: Cistercian Publications, 1994.

Dulles, Avery. *Models of the Church.* New York: Doubleday, 2022.

Faggioli, Massimo. "From Collegiality to Synodality: Promise and Limits of Francis's 'Listening Primacy.'" *Irish Theological Quarterly* 85 (2020): 352–69.

Faggioli, Massimo. *The Liminal Papacy of Pope Francis: Moving toward Global Catholicism.* Maryknoll, NY: Orbis, 2020.

Fraga, Brian. "Vatican's New Synod Document Draws Praise for Its Signs of Listening." *National Catholic Reporter.* October 27, 2022. https://www.ncronline.org/news/vaticans-new-synod-document-draws-praise-its-signs-listening.

Gaillardetz, Richard. "Loving and Reforming a Holy Yet Broken Church: My Last Lecture." *Worship* 97 (2023): 62–81.

Galli, Carlos María. "Revolución de la ternura y reforma de la iglesia." In *Reforma de estructuras y conversión de mentalidades. Retos y desafíos para una Iglesia Sinodal*, edited by Rafael Luciani and Carlos Federico Schickendantz, 55–92. Madrid: Khaf, 2020.

Glendinning, Chad J. "Structures of Accountability in the Parish and Diocese: Lessons Learned in North America and Possibilities for Reform." *Studia Canonica* 56 (2022): 645–69.

Grieu, Étienne. "Les plus pauvres au cœur de l'Église?" In *Les derniers seront les premiers: La parole des pauvres au coeur de la synodalité*, edited by François Odinet, 32–50. Paris: Éditions de l'Emmanuel, 2022.

Gruber, Judith. "Consensus or Dissensus? Exploring the Theological Role of Conflict in a Synodal Church." *Louvain Studies* 43 (2020): 239–59.

Hahnenberg, Edward. "The Mystical Body of Christ and Communion Ecclesiology: Historical Parallels." *Irish Theological Quarterly* 70 (2005): 3–30.

Horner, Jennifer Mechtild. "Listening with the Ear of the Heart: The Rule of Benedict and Synodality." *Monastic Bulletin* 123 (2022): 23–28.

Herman, Carolyn Weir. "What the Synod Doc Says about Women, and What It Could Mean for the Future of the Church." *America*. May 12, 2023. https://www.americamagazine.org/faith/2023/05/12/synodality-women-church-herman-245208.

Ignatius of Loyola. *The Spiritual Exercises*. In *Saint Ignatius of Loyola: Personal Writings*, translated by Joseph A. Muñitiz and Philip Endean. London: Penguin, 1996.

Ilo, Stan Chu. "The African Palaver Method: A Model Synodal Process for Today's Church." *Concilium* (2021/2): 68–76.

Ivereigh, Austen. *The Great Reformer: Francis and the Making of a Radical Pope*. New York: Henry Holt, 2014.

Ivereigh, Austen. "Hearing the Spirit in the Assembly of the People: Pope Francis's Vision of Synodality." *Studium: Rivista bimestrale di cultura* 117 (2021): 357–70.

Ivereigh, Austen. "I Helped Write the First Global Synod Document: Here's What We Heard from Catholics around the World." *America*. October 27, 2022. https://www.americamagazine.org/faith/2022/10/27/frascati-document-synod-synodality-244031.

Ivereigh, Austen. *Let Us Dream: The Path to a Better Future*. London: Simon & Schuster, 2020.

Ivereigh, Austen. *Wounded Shepherd: Pope Francis and His Struggle to Convert the Catholic Church*. New York: Henry Holt, 2019.

Join-Lambert, Arnaud. "Les liturgies synodales comme lieu ecclésiologique." *La Maison-Dieu* 287 (2017): 113–36.

Kennedy, Robert T. "Shared Responsibility in Ecclesial Decision Making." *Studia Canonica* 14 (1980): 5–23.

Klöckener, Martin. "La prière d'ouverture des conciles 'Adsumus': de l'Espagne wisigothique à la liturgie Romaine d'après Vatican II." In *La prière liturgique: Conférences Saint-Serge*, edited by Achille M. Triacca and Alessandro Pistoia, 165–98. Rome: Edizione Liturgiche, 2001.

Legrand, Hervé. "Communio Ecclesiae, Communio Ecclesiarum, Collegium Episcoporum." In *For a Missionary Reform of the Church: The* Civiltà Cattolica *Seminar*, edited by Antonio Spadaro and Carlos Maria Galli, 159–95. Mahwah, NJ: Paulist Press, 2017.

Liedel, Jonathan. "New 'Grammar of Synodality' on Display at the Start of Synod Gathering." Catholic News Agency. October 4,

2023. https://www.catholicnewsagency.com/news/255577/new
-grammar-of-synodality-on-display-at-start-of-synod-gathering.

Luciani, Rafael. *El Papa Francisco y la teología del pueblo*. Madrid: PPC, 2016.

Luciani, Rafael. "La *restitutio* al pueblo de Dios latinoamericano y caribeño: 'Lo que afecta a todos debe ser tratado y aprobado por todos.'" *Revista CLAR* 61/2 (2023): 14–29.

Luciani, Rafael. *Synodality: A New Way of Proceeding in the Church*. New York: Paulist Press, 2022.

Malvaux, Benoît. "Le pouvoir délibératif dans la compagnie de Jésus: la lettre et l'esprit." In *Délibérer en Église*, edited by Alphonse Borras, 89–110. Brussels: Lessius, 2010.

Mangnus, Stefan. "Dominican Gifts for a Synodal Church." In *Witnesses of Synodality: Good Practices and Experiences*, edited by Jos Moons, 14–26. Mahwah, NJ: Paulist Press, 2024.

Mares, Courtney. "Pope Francis Tells Latin American Ecclesial Assembly Not to Be Elitist." Catholic News Agency. January 25, 2021. https://www.catholicnewsagency.com/news/246229 /pope-francis-tells-latin-american-ecclesial-assembly-not-to-be -elitist.

Moons, Jos. *The Art of Spiritual Direction: A Guide to Ignatian Practice*. New York: Paulist Press, 2021.

Moons, Jos. "Broadening the Baptismal Foundation of a Synodal Church: A Plea for a Baptismal Ethos." *Studia Canonica* 58 (2024): 131–52.

Moons, Jos. "A Comprehensive Introduction to Synodality: Reconfiguring Ecclesiology and Ecclesial Practice." *Roczniki Teologiczne (Annals of Theology)* 69/2 (2022): 73–93.

Moons, Jos. "The Holy Spirit as the Protagonist of the Synod: Pope Francis's Creative Reception of the Second Vatican Council." *Theological Studies* 84/1 (2023): 61–78.

Moons, Jos. *The Holy Spirit, the Church, and Pneumatological Renewal:* Mystici Corporis, Lumen Gentium *and Beyond*. Leiden and Boston: Brill, 2022.

Moons, Jos. "La lettre ou l'esprit? La synodalité et les limites de la réforme du droit canon." *Nouvelle Revue Théologique* 145 (2023): 403–19.

Moons, Jos. "Synodality and Discernment: The Affective Reconfiguration of the Church." *Studia Canonica* 56 (2022): 379–93.

Moons, Jos. "A Weakness Exposed: Theologians on the Practice of Synodality." In *Theology Responding to the Challenge of Synodality: Proceedings of International Conference Held at the Pontifical Gregorian University (Rome, 27–29 April 2023)*, edited by Nathalie Becquart and Philipp Renczes, 463–70. Rome: Libreria Editrice Vaticana, 2024.

Moons, Jos, ed. *Witnesses of Synodality: Good Practices and Experiences.* Mahwah, NJ: Paulist Press, 2024.

Moons, Jos, and Robert Alvarez. *Theological Briefing Papers for the Synod 2023.* https://www.synodresources.org/newsletter_post/theological-briefing-papers-for-the-synod-assembly-2023/.

Noceti, Serena. *Reforming the Church: A Synodal Way of Proceeding.* New York: Paulist Press, 2023.

O'Collins, Gerald, with John Wilkins. *Lost in Translation: The English Language and the Catholic Mass.* Collegeville, MN: Liturgical Press, 2017.

O'Connell, Gerard. *The Election of Pope Francis: An Inside Account of the Conclave That Changed History.* Maryknoll, NY: Orbis, 2019.

O'Malley, John. "Vatican II: Did Anything Happen?" *Theological Studies* 67/1 (2006): 3–33.

O'Malley, John. *When Bishops Meet: An Essay Comparing Trent, Vatican I, and Vatican II.* Cambridge: Harvard University Press, 2019.

Ortega y Alamino, Jorge. "Aparecida y Evangelii Gaudium en esta hora de la Iglesia." *Revista Investigación y Pensamiento Crítico* 2/5 (September–December 2014): 99–108.

Plattig, Michael. "Gehorsam: Grundhaltung für synodale Prozesse." In *Synodalisierung: Eine Zerreißprobe für die katholische Weltkirche? Expertinnen und Experten aus aller Welt beziehen Stellung,* edited by Paul Zulehner, Peter Neuner, and Anna Hennersperger, 87–104. Ostfildern: Grünewald, 2022.

Polan, Gregory J. "Synodal Elements in the Rule of St. Benedict." *The American Benedictine Review* 73 (2022): 1–9.

Pottmeyer, Hermann J. *Towards a Papacy in Communion: Perspectives from Vatican Councils I & II*. New York: Herder and Herder, 1998.

Pulikkan, Paul. "Learning from Different Synodal Experiences (Council of Aparecida, Der Synodale Weg, Querida Amazonia, and Palliyogam)." *Encounter* 12 (2021): 41–58.

Radcliffe, Timothy. "Accountability and Co-Responsibility of the Church: The Example of the Dominicans." *Studia Canonica* 56 (2022): 587–604.

Radcliffe, Timothy. *Listening Together: Meditations on Synodality*. Collegeville, MN: Liturgical Press, 2024.

Reis, Bernadette M. "Synod Continental Stage: 'Most Innovative Aspect of Synodal Process.'" Vatican News. https://www.vatican news.va/en/vatican-city/news/2023-04/synod-continental-stage -conclusion-press-conference.html.

Reynolds, Susan Bigelow. "Are We Protagonists Yet? The Place of Women in the Synod's Working Document." *Commonweal*. December 9, 2022. https://www.commonwealmagazine.org/women -church-synod-francis-catholic.

Rohmer, Céline. "De la tradition synodale à l'événement synodal: ou comment la Bible interroge la Pratique." *Recherches de Science Religieuse* 107 (2019): 209–24.

Rosenberg, Randall S. "Cultivating a Synodal Disposition in Theological Education." In *Theology Responding to the Challenge of Synodality: Proceedings of International Conference Held at the Pontifical Gregorian University (Rome, 27–29 April 2023)*, edited by Nathalie Becquart and Philipp Renczes, 333–45. Rome: Libreria Editrice Vaticana, 2024.

Rowlands, Anna. "The Synod Has Taught Me Catholics Are Not as Divided as the Skeptics Thought." *America*. June 29, 2023. https://www.americamagazine.org/faith/2023/06/29/synod -synodality-polarization-lessons-245554.

Rush, Ormond. "Inverting the Pyramid: The *Sensus Fidelium* in a Synodal Church." *Theological Studies* 78 (2017): 299–325.

Rush, Ormond. *The Vision of Vatican II: Its Fundamental Principles*. Collegeville, MN: Liturgical Press, 2019.

Schenk, Christine. "When a Female Lens Is Added to the Equation, Something New Can Happen." *National Catholic Reporter*. May

9, 2023. https://www.ncronline.org/opinion/ncr-voices/when
-female-lens-added-equation-something-new-can-happen.

Silber, Stefan. "Synodalität als ekklesiologisches Prinzip ad intra und
ad extra: Lernen von der Bischofssynode für Amazonien."
Zeitschrift für Missionswissenschaft und Religionswissenschaft
105 (2021): 34–47.

Spadaro, Antonio. "A Big Heart Open to God: An Interview with
Pope Francis." *America*. September 30, 2013. https://www
.americamagazine.org/faith/2013/09/30/big-heart-open-god
-interview-pope-francis.

Spadaro, Antonio, and Carlos Maria Galli, eds. *For a Missionary
Reform of the Church: The* Civiltà Cattolica *Seminar*. Mahwah,
NJ: Paulist Press, 2017.

Theobald, Christoph. *Le courage de penser l'avenir: Études œcuméniques de theologies fondamentale et ecclésiologique*. Paris: Cerf,
2021.

Thibodeaux, Mark. *Reimagining the Ignatian Examen: Fresh Ways
to Pray from Your Day*. Chicago: Loyola Press, 2015.

Trigo, Pedro. "Synodality with the People: A Latin American Perspective." In *Reforming the Church: Global Perspectives*, edited
by Declan Marmion and Salvador Ryan, 113–34. Collegeville,
MN: Liturgical Press, 2023.

Tück, Jan-Heiner. "Sakrament des Heils für die Welt: Annäherungen
an einen ekklesiologischen Leitbegriff des Konzils." In *Die großen
Metaphern des Zweiten Vatikanischen Konzils: Ihre Bedeutung für
heute*, edited by Mariano Delgado and Michael Sievernich, 141–
67. Freiburg: Herder, 2013.

Ward, Benedicta. *The Sayings of the Desert Fathers*. Kalamazoo, MI:
Cistercian Publications, 1975.

Weiler, Birgit. "Synodality in Continental Perspective: Latin America
and the Caribbean." In *Witnesses of Synodality: Good Practices
and Experiences*, edited by Jos Moons, 131–44. Mahwah, NJ:
Paulist Press, 2024.

Wijlens, Myriam. "'The Church of God Is Convoked in Synod':
Theological and Canonical Challenges Concerning the 2021–2023
Synod." *Centro Pro Unione Semi-Annual Bulletin* 100 (2021):
86–106.

Wijlens, Myriam. "Reforming the Church by Hitting the Reset Button: Reconfiguring Collegiality within Synodality because of *sensus fidei fidelium.*" *The Canonist* 8 (2017): 235–61.

Wijlens, Myriam, and Vimal Tirimanna, eds. *The People of God Have Spoken: Continental Ecclesial Assemblies with the Synod on Synodality.* Dublin: Columba Books, 2023.

Willekes, Rebekka. "Synodal Wisdom from the Rule of Benedict." In *Witnesses of Synodality: Good Practices and Experiences*, edited by Jos Moons, 1–13. Mahwah, NJ: Paulist Press, 2024.

Winters, Sean. "Synodal Working Document Is Deeply Rooted in Vatican II." *National Catholic Reporter.* June 26, 2023. https://www.ncronline.org/opinion/ncr-voices/synodal-working-document-deeply-rooted-vatican-ii.

Wood, Susan, ed. *Ordering the Baptismal Priesthood: Theologies of Lay and Ordained Ministry.* Collegeville, MN: Liturgical Press, 2003.